Cathedrals of Kudzu

M

Cathedrals of Kudzu

a personal landscape of the south

HAL CROWTHER

Foreword by FRED HOBSON
Illustrations by STEVEN CRAGG

Louisiana State University Press

Baton Rouge MM

Designer: Barbara Neely Bourgoyne
Typeface: Adobe Garamond
Printer and binder: Thomson-Shore, Inc.

Library of Congress Cataloging-in-Publication Data
Crowther, Hal.
    Cathedrals of kudzu : a personal landscape of the South : essays / by Hal Crowther ;
foreword by Fred Hobson.
        p. cm.
    ISBN 0-8071-2594-6 (cloth); ISBN 0-8071-2788-4 (pbk.)
    1. Southern States—Civilization. 2. Southern States—Social conditions. 3. Southern
States—Intellectual life. 4. American literature—Southern States—History and criticism.
5. United States—Civilization—1970– 6. United States—Social conditions—1980–
7. United States—Intellectual life. I. Title.

F209 .C78 2000
975—dc21

                                                                                    00-037112

The author offers grateful acknowledgment to Marc Smirnoff, John Grisham, and the editorial staff of the *Oxford American*, where most of these essays originally appeared. Thanks also
to Michael Skube of the *Atlanta Journal-Constitution*, to Steve Schewel of the *Independent
Weekly*, and to the editors at the *Spectator*, who published the others. Special thanks to Fred
Hobson, Andrea Blair, John Sullivan, Lee Smith, Mona Sinquefield, and Carol Collier Wills.

The photograph used on the endsheets is by Nancy Marshall and is titled *Near Cartersville,
Georgia* (8 inches × 20 inches, silver print toned), © 2000 by Nancy Marshall.

The illustrations of James Dickey, Stonewall Jackson, Pat Robertson, and Doc Watson on
pages 2, 56, 104, and 150 are copyright © 2000 by Steven Cragg.

The paper in this book meets the guidelines for permanence and durability of the Committee on Production Guidelines for Book Longevity of the Council on Library Resources. ∞

For Amity, my Southern daughter

The South would not have been defeated had it possessed a sufficient faith in its own kind of God.

—Allen Tate, *I'll Take My Stand*

The world is a strange place and in it lie things of another nature, a bent order, and beyond a certain point there are no rules to make men mind.

—Larry Brown, "A Roadside Resurrection"

Contents

Foreword

Fred Hobson

A few years ago, in the early 1990s, I was a judge in the competition for the H. L. Mencken Award, given annually by the Baltimore Sun-papers to an American journalist who captures, if only in a minor key, something of the spirit and style of that earlier iconoclast. Hal Crowther had won the award the previous year, and I assumed I would find—among the ninety or so contestants—at least two or three writers who were in his league. I found no one remotely close. We gave the award to someone, but I was astounded by the mediocrity and superficiality of most of the writing. It made me realize how really good Crowther is. I can't think of an American newspaper or magazine columnist who is better—that is, as a *writer*—no one who has the ear for language, for speech rhythms, for cadences, no one who can make prose sing and dance as he can.

Crowther in many ways is a throwback: that is, he writes like many of the best literary journalists of the first third of the century—W. J. Cash, Gerald W. Johnson, Mencken himself. First, he has read widely, and he has a store of classical and literary allusions that very, very few contemporary journalists have at their command. He writes with a sense of the absurd, the ironic, the mock-epic; he takes his seat as a particularly delighted spectator of the human comedy. He has a *voice,* he creates a persona. Writing to him is more than a vehicle for con-veying information—although that gets done. But, again, he makes prose stand up and do tricks. And he also has something to say, has a distinctive point of view, and (again somewhat like Mencken and earlier journalists) doesn't mind offending people. And offend them he does. I live in central North Carolina, where Crowther's column over the years has appeared in the *Independent Weekly*. During the time I've read the column, I have seen Crowther assaulted by readers left and right, disbelievers and footwashing fundamentalists, feminists and male traditionalists. His own politics, in general, seem to be something like Old Liberal, politics formed very much by the decade of the 1960s, but thrown into the mix is the patrician Eastern Republicanism of Crowther's own youth (Javits, Keating, Lindsay—a time and place when Republicans could be something other than reactionary yahoos) and a keen awareness of necessary social changes since that time. Crowther is—in the best sense of that often abused word—a moralist (as all the best essayists, at base, are), an idealist even, holding his own idea of the good society and filled with indignation when he views the carnival of bad taste and bad ethics and charlatan religion masquerading as respectable in contemporary American society.

In the pieces included in this collection Crowther ranges from contemporary culture to American—and particularly southern—letters. In fact, all of these essays, in some fashion, comment on the American South—which makes, I guess, *Cathedrals of Kudzu* an appropriate title. Among my favorite of the essays are "The Last Wolverine," his tribute to the late poet James Dickey; "In Stonewall's Shadow," a meditation on John Brown, the Late Confederacy, and Old Virginia; and "Father, Forgive Me," a discourse on fathers and sons. But I could add a dozen more as well.

I say Crowther can make the language sing and dance. Take, for example, his description of twentieth-century Dixie's maddest bard: "Dickey raged up out of Georgia like an unstable air mass, a sudden storm that blows the windows open. 'Class dismissed,' snarled those outlaw bikers, bullwhip Baptists, and carnivorous mammals who stalked his violent verse. When life was all possibility and poetry seemed indispensable, *Poems, 1957–1967* was my Bible. I still own the original paperback, that thick green volume with a cherubic Dickey on the cover, in his button-down shirt and tie. Nearly every page is separated from the binding now and half of them are stained with red wine, which I know he'd appreciate."

Or of the inescapable presence of race in the American psyche: "Race is like a big crazy cousin locked in the basement, a red-eyed giant who strangled a dog and crippled a policeman the last time he got loose. We never forget that he's down there. But it's amazing how long we can ignore him, no matter how much noise he makes moaning and banging on the pipes. Our denial's almost airtight, until one day he's out in the yard again swinging a pickax, and all we can do is blame each other and dial 911."

Or (before the Know-Nothings of the Right discovered it as a target), on political correctness: "The creeping curse of political correctness establishes its regional beachheads at universities, where traditions of free speech and academic freedom protect the learned men and women who expose students to uncommon, unpopular ideas—where tenured scholars who drive BMWs dispense Marxist theories that have long since vanished from the playing fields of history. . . . [Political correctness is] the fascism of the Left, the orthodoxy of lame time-servers, the detritus that piles up where small minds and half-baked principles collide with real social change. For paleo-liberals like me, it's anathema."

Or, finally, on poetry: "In the best poetry the words are breathing . . . and they manufacture ghosts and pictures. Real poetry is luminous and numinous, but best of all it's precise. In the best hands, its precision is awesome. Novelists release floods of words and then go back over them like inspectors on an assembly line, looking for defects and duds. Journalists choose their words as carefully as they can, under the circumstances, under the clock. But a gifted poet in his pride will never release a word he's ashamed of, and his best choices can cut like a laser."

Crowther holds forth, then, on a variety of subjects—Southern Gothic, unreconstructed southerners, New Orleans, long-distance driving, southern evangelists ("Of all the utter nonsense that has been uttered since the dawn of speech . . . nine-tenths has been uttered into microphones in rural America in the past thirty years, in the name of Jesus Christ"), dogs ("the hounds of heaven"), trees, God and evil, southern belles ("If 'the flower of Southern womanhood' sprang from a dark soil mulched with racism, testosterone, and guilt, does that make it wrong to admire the blossoms?"), lying-in-the-road deaths, and law and order—as well as (besides Dickey) Erskine Caldwell, Cormac McCarthy, George Wallace, Frank Johnson (Wallace's adversary in the morality play that was 1960s Alabama), Elvis and Doc Watson. Even Crowther's throwaway lines are often gems, for example, his observation, in passing, on the phenomenon of millions of Americans, in internet chat rooms, mourning the death of JFK Jr.—"a glutinous mass of media slaves mourning a man they never met with people they've never seen."

Enough. Suffice it to say that Crowther may be the sanest social commentator on the American South (and on numerous other parts of the Republic) since Walker Percy. He has something to say, and he says in language that performs before your eyes.

I

THE PEN

This Is Our Swamp

The Last Wolverine

James Dickey (1923–1997)

At his memorial service, they all said he was bigger than life. He was definitely bigger than me. For a prosemonger, I seem to have met a host of poets; James Dickey was the only one who ever clamped me in a headlock I couldn't break.

It was a cruel introduction to genius. Dickey was my literary idol. His poetry, beginning with the publication of *May Day Sermon to the Women of Gilmer County, Georgia, by a Woman Preacher Leaving the Baptist Church,* broke a grade-school spell cast by T. S. Eliot and bloodless sages writing dirges in the dark, sipping weak tea, and waiting for the end.

Dickey raged up out of Georgia like an unstable air mass, a sudden storm that blows the windows open. "Class dismissed," snarled those outlaw bikers, bullwhip Baptists, and carnivorous mammals who stalked his violent verse. When life was all possibility and poetry seemed indispensable, *Poems, 1957–1967* was my Bible. I still own the original paperback, that thick green volume with a cherubic Dickey on the cover, in his button-down shirt and tie. Nearly every page is separated from the binding now and half of them are stained with red wine, which I know he'd appreciate.

I met the poet in 1969, in the prime of his career. I'd organized a poetry contest for employees of Time, Inc. Someone at *Life* talked Dickey into judging the finalists and flying up to New York to grace the presentations. I was awed at the prospect of meeting him and delighted with his choices—third prize for my girlfriend and first prize to *Time* proofreader Susan Mitchell, who submitted a remarkable poem (she was later a finalist for the National Book Award in poetry).

Joy reigned through Dickey's reading of Susan's poem. I wanted these New Yorkers to hear a true poet read in the drawl they associated with George Wallace and Lester Maddox. Dickey was superb, but I noticed that his bottle of Jack Daniel's was half empty. The whiskey was below the label when he said something sexually explicit—menacing, actually—to the prizewinner; the bottle was empty when he seized me in a headlock that all but turned out my lights.

When Dickey lost interest in killing me, I lurched free and noticed that the editors and executives had left the reception. My story gets worse, in some ways, but the gory details are generic. A lot of poetry lovers were tested by these performances. Nearly twenty years later I worked up the courage to remind him of our first encounter. The only thing Dickey could remember was Susan Mitchell's poem.

It was Dickey who established, at least for the Southern circuit, the notorious *droit d'écrivain*—the unwritten law that for all women who attend literary events, the sexual claims of a visiting writer take precedence over any previous relationships, including marriage. He seemed honestly, innocently surprised when a woman or her escort failed to recognize his claim. At one women's college they still tell the story of a friend of mine who narrowly escaped Dickey's ursine advances through a ruse ("Let me run up and get a nightie, Jim") and left him baying dolefully beneath her dormitory window—"Ciiiindy . . . Ciiiindy"—until the night watchmen led him away.

It goes back to the troubadours, this sexual indulgence of poets, this convention that they live by laws of their own. It's inherently offensive, especially when it's exploited by charlatans and bad poets.

It could only be justified by genius. James Dickey was an unruly, unreliable, impossible man. He was a shambling 220-pound dissertation on the theme "poetic license," a true connoisseur of excess. Yet most of the people he embarrassed, frightened, or compromised managed to forgive him long before he died. Some people couldn't understand Lynn Redgrave's character in the movie *Shine*, when she drops an investment banker to marry pianist David Helfgott, a bizarre schizophrenic. But who with an atom of soul wouldn't try to love a man who could play—or write—so well?

Dickey believed, to a dangerous degree, that art justified everything. There was no point in accusing him of calculation. His act was an inseparable part of his art, and like the poems it wasn't always lovely to behold.

"They don't make men like Jim Dickey anymore," said novelist Pat Conroy, one of Dickey's eulogists. It's obvious that this is true, not half so obvious *why* it's true. Dickey was a sensual, willful man who had close brushes with death when he was very young, flying combat missions with the 418th Night Fighter Squadron in the Pacific. Defining himself as a survivor, he committed his life to a relentless, sometimes reckless pursuit of unmediated experience.

More often than any other poet, more skillfully than any other, he answered the question, "What does it feel like?" What does it feel like to be a living creature in its skin—in pain, in ecstasy, in terror, in a state of grace? He entered the skins of animals so convincingly, it's a nice conceit to imagine that he's gone, by choice, to "The Heaven of Animals" he created:

> For some of these,
> It could not be the place
> It is, without blood.
> These hunt, as they have done,
> With claws and teeth grown perfect

As the earthbound understand it, the poetic imagination comes with wings; only Dickey's came equipped with talons, too. In a fallen world where our worst instinct, our herd instinct, is reinforced and manipulated to make consumers and networkers of us all, Dickey followed more ancient instincts. He was a solitary predator—a big cat consumed with curiosity—who made up his own menu as he went along.

It was an impressive menu, unless you were on it. A member of Dickey's family thanked Pat Conroy for glossing over the poet's legendary "appetites." But without the appetites, could we have had the poems? As Dickey himself wrote, in the stunning, bravura "For the Last Wolverine"—

> How much the timid poem needs
> The mindless explosion of your rage
> The glutton's internal fire . . .

James Dickey ate more than his share and never apologized. He was no respecter of persons, of marriage vows, of middle-class morals. He was a harsh and brilliant critic whose humility and charity often failed him. No one should be ashamed of failing to like him—only for failing to appreciate what he could do.

A great poet is defined by his antagonists; Dickey collected his enemies as judiciously as he chose his words. Poetry attracts more than its share of Prufrocks, head-dwellers uncomfortable in their skin, city mice petrified of poison ivy and insects. Naturally they detested Dickey, the doubly blessed, who lived so intensely in his skin as well as in his head. Naturally they begrudged him his laurels.

It's fitting that his nemesis was Robert Bly, of *Iron John* fame, who for years has earned a living teaching America's Prufrocks how to reach the Wild Man inside themselves. What a priceless irony, Bly's housebroken males struggling to locate their Wild Men while Dickey received delegations beseeching him to keep his own Wild Man chained in the basement.

Bly called him "a huge blubbery poet," a wide miss on all counts to anyone who read Dickey, or wrestled him. Bly isn't always such a fool. But he was no match for James Dickey, neither on the page nor arm-wrestling bard to bard, a showdown Dickey would have given his last caesura to arrange.

Dickey disliked Eliot, dismissed the Beat poets as clowns, and disparaged "the school of Gabby Agony" epitomized by Sylvia Plath and

Anne Sexton. To the frustration of his friends and partisans, he backed down from a fight about as readily as his wolverine, and he paid the price.

Between the animus of the poetry establishment, the literary world's generic condescension to Southerners, and the incomprehension of ponderous philistines like Jonathan Yardley of the *Washington Post,* Dickey usually found himself paddling upstream. Fortunately he relished such uncloistered, high-visibility assignments as the space program (he was the first "poet of space"), the Jimmy Carter inauguration, and the Hollywood film of his novel *Deliverance.* They made him a famous man. Yet American poetry did not thrive, or hold its own, in his time. He may be the last poet honored with a six-column obituary in the *New York Times.*

"The world doesn't esteem us very much," he told his last class at the University of South Carolina, "but we are masters of a superior secret."

The handful of poets at the memorial service in Columbia acknowledged the full irony of the last line of "For the Last Wolverine," printed on the program: "Lord, let me die, but not die out."

Poetry is a small world where Dickey's death leaves a huge hole, with no candidates to fill it. But the beauty of a great poet is that he leaves himself a thousand perfect epitaphs, embracing every possibility of death and resurrection. Here are the last lines of his last novel, *To the White Sea:* "I was in it, and part of it. I matched it all. And I will be everywhere in it from now on. You will be able to hear me, just like you're hearing me now. Everywhere in it, for the first time and the last, as soon as I close my eyes."

Yes.

Cathedrals of Kudzu

Southern Gothic, a literary sampler:

> What was left of him, rotted beneath what was left of the nightshirt, had become inextricable from the bed in which he lay; and upon him and upon the pillow beside him lay that even coating of the patient and biding dust.
>
> —William Faulkner, "A Rose for Emily," 1924

> When she was disinterred some weeks later, upon the intervention of a young man whom she had never loved, it was found that the flesh, upon which so many lovers had tendered caresses in every conceivable variation of passion, wonder, gentleness and lust . . . had reached such an advanced state of putrefaction in Potter's Field (it was August) that the authorities considered for a moment the advisability of leaving the body there to resume its process of gradual, anonymous decay.
>
> —William Styron, first draft of *Lie Down in Darkness,* 1947

> The rope drew taut and the first of the dead sat up on the cave floor, the hands that hauled the rope above sorting the shadows like puppeteers. Gray soapy clots of matter fell from the cadaver's chin. She ascended dangling. She sloughed in the weem of the noose. A gray rheum dripped.
>
> —Cormac McCarthy, *Child of God,* 1973

> Sometime during the night somebody had pinned the monkey to the bar with an ice pick through the thorax and it lay there atrophied with its palms upward like Christ in its final agony. Several people had put out cigarettes on it. Somebody had bought it a drink. Somebody had cut off its tail.
>
> —Larry Brown, *Father and Son,* 1996

"Gothic" isn't the easiest word to define, but most of us know Gothic when we see it. If our best Southern writers are downright cozy with the odd cadaver and not at all squeamish about decomposition, is there something about the South that made them that way?

It seems clear that Mary Shelley wrote *Frankenstein* and Percy Shelley wrote the lurid Gothic romances *Zastrozzi* and *St. Irvyne* (before he turned twenty) because they belonged to a community, an archetypal writers' support group that shared its nightmares.

There was nothing like that to spur these Southerners. Most of them wrote in notorious isolation. W. J. Cash theorized that all Southerners take in violence with the air they breathe, and that after The War it became a toxic vapor compounded of violence and defeat. Would that account adequately for Edgar Allan Poe, the Southerner who defined American Gothic with "The Fall of the House of Usher," or for Faulkner who defined Southern Gothic with "A Rose for Emily"? Would it account for Flannery O'Connor or Cormac McCarthy?

Webster's Collegiate defines "Gothic" as "of or relating to a style of fiction characterized by the use of desolate or remote settings and macabre, mysterious, or violent incidents." That dances around a central Gothic convention, that you can't get it done outdoors. Storms, wave-lashed cliffs, lights in the swamp or voices in the forest may help to set a mood, but when the sun comes out and the hard hot light hits it, Gothic has always had to run home and bolt the door behind it. High Gothic was inseparable from old houses and the kind of people who were alleged to inhabit them.

Architecture is one key to the Gothic imagination. The world the Shelleys inhabited was still rich in castles, abbeys, tombs, and ruins, and the South of their literary descendants could boast great gloomy structures of its own. In every Southern village there was at least one house that collected stories and frightened children.

We still catch an occasional glimpse of what they used to mean when they said "Southern Gothic." There's the house in Milledgeville, Georgia, where Flannery O'Connor's ancient mother lived, with the yard so overgrown you couldn't see the ground, and the back rooms in such a neglected condition that a vine had entered through a broken window and twisted off into some dark bedchamber where the dust and mildew lay heavy as a rug. What lurks inside such a place we can only imagine, until the last heir dies and the wrecker's ball erases two hundred years of mystery in a single afternoon.

On just one occasion a door opened for me and I stepped into Southern Gothic as an invited guest. It was a huge and tastefully decrepit white brick mansion in New Orleans, owned by a tall, stagy gentleman who was once in politics. He led me into a dining room straight out of *Nosferatu,* and with a sweep of his arm, indicating tapestries, carved panels, and choir-stall chairs that looked more medieval than antique, he said, "None of these have anything to do with my family. They're all from auctions and dealers. This house is just a monument to my father's ego."

In a parlor forty feet long and nearly as high, he seated himself on the grandfather of all leather sofas and in a confidential voice shared some paranoid worldview that seemed to demonize Jews and exalt women. I offered no response. I'd strayed into a story where I didn't belong, where I didn't know any of my lines. His ex-wife, my escort, stared at him as if he might pull a bell rope and bring this whole House of Usher down around us, complete with mad sister screaming in the hallway.

I don't know anything about furniture, but I know an original when I see one. This guy had it all. Gothicism has flourished wherever there was a boundless tolerance for secrecy and eccentricity, a genetic predisposition toward violence and morbidity—*and,* above all, the stage props to bring it off.

Today it's the props that are in short supply—the big ruined houses, sinister portraits in gilt frames, overgrown mausoleums, canopied avenues of live oaks where the sun never shines. There's no question the South has changed. The question is whether Southerners have changed, or changed the furniture of their imaginations.

Not as much as you might expect. If literature is any guide, Southern Gothic has survived—triumphantly—its loss of habitat and a drastic reduction in the pool of decadent aristocrats who used to take its leading roles.

Faulkner, early on and often, took his show out of town and away from the big houses. Flannery O'Connor proved that pedigrees and historical backlighting were superfluous, that monsters and mysteries could spring right out of the red clay at our feet. Cormac McCarthy moved Gothic out-of-doors with a vengeance, though his landscapes owe more to Poe's "ghoul-haunted woodland of Weir" than to anything I've seen in Mississippi or Tennessee.

Today the future of Southern Gothic appears to be in the capable hands of a pair of novelists from Mississippi. Lewis Nordan *(Wolf Whistle, Music of the Swamp, Sharpshooter Blues)*, a stylist second to none, sets his fiction in a mythical Delta that's about half Mississippi and half Macondo, the haunted kingdom of Gabriel Garcia Marquez.

Oxford's Larry Brown *(Dirty Work, Joe, Father and Son)* has moved High Gothic to the other side of the tracks, once and for all—out to the pickup trucks and mobile homes, the rundown apartment buildings and four-room cabins packed with dogs and children. Out along the roadside in the open air, where he sets the deliberately outrageous story "A Roadside Resurrection," packed with "everything I could get in here: Jesus, Elvis, faith healers, overweight women, incest, truckers, goats, pistols, sin and faith and redemption."

There's a line in it Poe would appreciate: "The world is a strange place and in it lie things of another nature, a bent order, and beyond a certain point there are no rules to make men mind."

That's the Gothic declaration of independence, if I ever read it anywhere. Snobs might use terms like "Redneck Gothic" or "Welfare Gothic" to put Brown in his place, or protest that the characters in Brown's fiction have never heard the word "Gothic" or read a Gothic novel, or any novel. But they're tin-eared snobs if they miss the power of these stories, or all the new possibilities for Southern fiction they suggest.

You read Brown and Nordan and you begin to see familiar things in a different light. Up in Hindman, Kentucky, I saw what I can only describe as a Gothic cathedral of kudzu, towers and arches and buttresses one hundred feet high, the vines covering huge trees and maybe buildings and cars and God knows what all, who would ever dare go in there and look? And one night on our mountain, at 3 A.M., I heard this terrible moaning foghorn sound, like the devil's own milkcow hung up in an electric fence. It went on for an hour, waking up every frightened soul and dog on Laurel Knob. In the morning we learned that it was the fire horn—someone had set fire to the drug dealer's house up on the ridge, burned it to the ground. Vigilantes, confederates, dissatisfied customers? No one knows.

That's the South, too. Southern Gothic will be alive—or more accurately, in existence—when the last antebellum mansion has crumbled into the kudzu and the last Temple Drake or Peyton Loftis has pierced her nose. We don't need marble crypts or moonlight to do Gothic, any more than good actors need balconies and ball gowns to do Shakespeare. We are just profoundly weird.

Strangers in the Swamp

Beyond the mountains was the North: the Land of the Damyankees, where live People Who Cause All of Our Trouble.

—Lillian Smith, *Killers of the Dream*

For anyone whose sensibilities were formed south or west of the Hudson River, publishing is and probably always will be an exasperating collaboration with semihostile aliens. Southerners suffer most from the collision of incompatible cultures. Since there's no route to national recognition that doesn't run through New York, Southern writers are obliged to grit their teeth and steer a course somewhere between hysterical Yankee-bashing and mute despair.

Lee Smith gets a lot of mileage out of the Greenwich Village copy editor who scrawled in the margin of her manuscript, "Double-wide what?" But the provincial ignorance of New York editors is no joke at all. At lunch with a book editor—a former *New Yorker* editor—I made the mistake of asking him which Southern writers he preferred. This influential editor, whom I know to be well educated and otherwise well informed, was unable to name a Southern writer—except for the author of a middlebrow "sisterhood" novel his house had recently published. In his world Eudora Welty and Cormac McCarthy might have been Kurds.

He was not embarrassed. Neither was the New York editor who paid his first visit to Mississippi last winter and came back raving about all the civilized people he met in Jackson, like a tourist amazed to see how many Sumatrans own TV sets. This is the Lincoln Tunnel-vision from which Louis Rubin, Jr., was trying to protect Southern writers when he launched Algonquin Books of Chapel Hill.

There's a narrow gate, fiercely guarded by clueless Islanders, that each Dixie-crafted manuscript must negotiate in order to reach a wider audience. What's more, literary Manhattan is exporting a deadly dogma that clouds the future of serious writing and reading like nothing since deconstruction.

North Carolina's Jill McCorkle filed this letter from the *New Yorker's* fiction editor in her jewelry box, where she keeps things she doesn't want to lose. "'Words Gone Bad,'" the editor writes, rejecting McCorkle's short story, "goes against an uncodified resistance here to narrators whose ethnicity differs from the writer's."

At least the *New Yorker* had the bravado to put it in writing. A few months later McCorkle found herself facing a panel of New York magazine editors, and asked them point-blank: "If you didn't know anything about me before you read this story, would you call me to make sure I was a black woman?"

McCorkle reports that a silence fell, followed by editors muttering and glancing at each other. She got no straight answer from any of them. Later she asked a friend, the fiction editor of a literary magazine. He admitted that he'd have made the race-checking call just as she imagined it.

"I'm insulted when writers do white Southerners badly, and they do that all the time," says McCorkle. "But are we supposed to be nasty even when someone does us well, just because he's not a native? John Dufresne, who wrote *Louisiana Power and Light*—he got the dialect perfectly. He's from Western Massachusetts."

Southern whites, of course, are not among the groups who are entitled to object when they're done badly, or imagined absurdly, by unskilled and prejudiced writers. Logic and evenhandedness were early casualties of the Cultural Revolution called "multiculturalism" or "cultural diversity" by its friends and "political correctness" by its enemies. In theory, these terms mean sensitivity to the feelings of women and minorities. In practice, they usually mean cringing submission to any identity group that's not made up of sexually orthodox white men with good jobs. In this absurd Balkanization of America, society's watchdogs have become its editors-in-chief.

Only the Left could produce humorless thought police who issue codes to regulate fiction. When Saul Bellow encountered the "uncodified resistance" that amazed McCorkle, he asked, incredulously, if that meant he should write only in the voices of old Jewish men from Chicago.

But PC is immune to irony, and its excess is no longer confined to New York and the ivory towers of the remote Northeast. Janice Daugharty saw the beast bare its teeth in Georgia, at a campus conference dedicated to women writers of the South. A black scholar waited until Daugharty left town, as the author tells it, and then condemned Daugharty's novel *Whistle* for breaking the Law of Ethnicity.

"She said I had no business writing in a black woman's voice, that I was stereotyping, that it's 'not my place,' to imagine a black woman," says Daugharty, a South Georgia writer small in stature but tall in spirit and attitude. "What kind of talk is that? I can't believe she actually read the book."

Pearl McHaney, who teaches at Georgia State and edits the *Eudora Welty Newsletter,* reports that even Deep South publishers are beginning to edit as if the chill hand of the culture vigilante were resting on their shoulders. The University Press of Mississippi was adamant about a couple of small changes in a memoir *(The Road to West 43rd Street,* 1995) by Welty's old friend Nash K. Burger, on which McHaney collaborated. One was the substitution of "little chocolate-flavored candies" for "nigger babies," a confection favored by Burger and Welty when they were children. McHaney protests that James Joyce's biographer Richard Ellmann, writing in pre-PC 1959, devoted half a page to Nora Barnacle Joyce's taste for "nigger babies."

But that was in another country. The creeping curse of political correctness establishes its regional beachheads at universities, where traditions of free speech and academic freedom protect the learned men and women who expose students to uncommon, unpopular ideas—where tenured scholars who drive BMWs dispense Marxist theories that have long since vanished from the playing fields of history. That's as it should be. But it's only since the dawn of "cultural diversity" that many of these exotic refugees have refused to extend the same freedoms that shelter them to people who disagree with them—students, colleagues, or visiting speakers. The notorious Stanley Fish, recently of Duke, not only rules out free speech in the academy but loves to engage defenders of free speech, myself included, in spirited debate.

From intimate exposure, I've developed a pathological loathing for political correctness. It's the fascism of the Left, the orthodoxy of lame time-servers, the detritus that piles up where small minds and half-baked principles collide with real social change. For paleo-liberals like me, it's anathema.

Is it as bad for America as the institutionalized racism and matter-of-fact misogyny, homophobia, and xenophobia it was intended to displace? Of course not. But it's just as bad—in some ways worse—for literature, history, journalism, or any discipline that pursues some form of the truth. Fundamentalist book-burners, who operate in a universe where no one reads much anyway, aren't half so great a threat to free expression. PC poisons *our* well. It corrupts from within, attacking the fragile ecosystem of people who make their living from the language.

"But this is our swamp," Pogo Possum used to say. Books are where we live, and PC vigilantes are an alien species we can't accommodate and hope to survive. And that goes more than double—triple, a hundred times—for the South. Of all the alien species that make a nuisance of themselves in the Southern biosphere—the flathead catfish, the balsam woolly adelgid, the Old World climbing fern—*PC censorious* is most comparable to *Myocastor coypus,* the relentless South American rodent that's over-running thousands of square miles of Deep South wetlands. *M. coypus,* better known as the nutria, is the one swamp critter you didn't encounter in *Pogo,* because he hadn't yet arrived when Walt Kelly was drawing the strip.

This is our swamp. The red clay is still raw on Jim Crow's grave; the deceased left wounds too deep to be healed by anything less than honesty, brutal honesty if necessary. Most white Southerners claim a living relative who once did something they'd rather not talk about. To give in to PC—to unreality, evasion, ivory-tower pharisaism—is as ugly as giving in to the prevalent see-no-evil, country-club bigotry that replaced open resistance to racial equality.

Southerners, and most of all Southern writers, are obliged to face the facts and never fudge them. (That's what Eudora Welty and Nora Joyce actually called the little candies, don't you see? No one is entitled to edit reality, no matter how distasteful, to save anyone's feelings.)

Name a more useful exercise, for the white Southern writer, than fiction that makes a sincere attempt to imagine the lives and views of African Americans. Name one with higher risks. Minority scholars and critics have the right, even the responsibility, to counterattack when they feel misrepresented or libeled. They have no right to make rules and post "No trespassing" signs for writers whose "ethnicity" is incorrect.

The gnawing nutria of political correctness has no place in our swamp, nothing to offer that we need. But the critters breed faster than the gators can eat them, and if they don't encounter more natural enemies it won't be our swamp much longer. Don't count on academics, who are often afflicted with security issues and herd instincts. Writers may be the South's last line of defense. Fortunately many of them are direct descendants, pychologically, of the stubborn rebels who held the line against the inevitable at Chickamauga.

Jill McCorkle—unbowed—is writing a new story narrated by the same black woman who offended the *New Yorker.* "This is a voice that's very much a part of my experience," she says, "and I'd be a fool to throw her away."

"I take any point of view I choose," declares Janice Daugharty, who lives just down the road from Pogo's beloved Okefenokee. "I'm writing a story in the voice of an old black lady who takes care of an invalid—and this is a mean, belligerent old lady. I knew her. I break their rules every day."

I sense a low level of intimidation. Next time you're on 43rd Street, tell them this war isn't over, either.

A Knight in White Flannel

The small town of American legend—of William Faulkner, Sherwood Anderson, Thornton Wilder, Edwin Arlington Robinson—has been in failing health for so long that its actual death will be declared arbitrarily, probably by a magazine writer, and no one will bother to argue. But two stories in the business pages—Woolworth's closing its last dime stores, Montgomery Ward declaring bankruptcy—take us close enough to the last breath to serve as obituaries.

According to the reporter, Montgomery Ward lost its share of the department-store market by refusing to move to suburban malls. And Wal-Mart, victorious, will never move back to town, not even to take over its defeated rivals' stores at a penny on the dollar. To build the kind of sprawling superstores that destroyed Main Street America and made the Waltons the royal family of retailing, you'd need to raze three city blocks. One Wal-Mart requires far more floor space than you could find in the entire business district of the town where I grew up.

Faulkner understood, maybe better than any other American writer, that there's tragedy on the business page and human destiny in the clash of economic forces. Montgomery Ward was founded in 1872, coincidentally the same year the novelist's great-grandfather, the ferocious Colonel W. C. Falkner, finished building the Ripley, Ship Island, and Kentucky Railroad that established the family fortune. William Faulkner's conniving, soulless Snopeses, descendants of a barn-burner, epitomized commercial enterprise without honor and the triumph of unprincipled avarice that anti-Semites like Ezra

Pound were blaming on the Jews. One of his most repugnant Snopeses was named Montgomery Ward—a bearded pornographer in a
beret who opens a shop in Jefferson called "Atelier Monty."

Faulkner played the Snopeses for comedy, comparing them to ro-
dents and insects and digressing at great length on the feral nature
and genetic shortcomings of "the true Snopes." But he was serious,
passionate and pessimistic about the threat they posed to every tradition that he held dear.

Faulkner, who died in 1962—three years after *The Mansion* com-
pleted his Snopes trilogy—probably thought he'd lived to see the final
victory of Snopesism in America. We know now, of course, that he
hadn't seen anything. We can consider whether the ghost-town mak-
ers, the Wal-Mart Waltons—from Arkansas across the river, where
Faulkner's characters always fled from disaster and dishonor—are true
Snopeses or just shrewd merchants molded by the marketplace they
found.

But what would Faulkner make of Bill Gates, the megaSnopes,
the cyberSnopes from Microsoft who devours whole industries (and
in his not-so-wild dreams whole societies of techno-captives) with a
ruthless singlemindedness that old Flem Snopes would have envied?

Faulkner grew up in the heyday of small-town America, near the
end of the bucolic half-century between Appomattox and Verdun
that some historians designate as our one Golden Age. Though he's associated, like Sinclair Lewis, with novels that exposed the hypocrisy
and meanness behind Main Street's innocent facade, Faulkner was
above all an idealist, a stubborn believer in the small-town virtues,
the human qualities all true Snopeses lack. He enumerates them as
"the verities of the human heart . . . courage, honor, pride, compassion, pity."

If the Hydra-headed Snopes is Jefferson's dragon, its St. George is
Gavin Stevens, Faulkner's most ubiquitous character and the one
many critics take as an idealized (and ironic) version of the author
himself. Faulkner doesn't do so well by Gavin Stevens. He has him
beaten and bloodied, in both *The Town* and *The Mansion*, protect-

ing women whose favors Stevens never wins; he enlists him to utter some of the most melodramatic, penny-dreadful dialogue anywhere in serious literature ("What we're trying to deal with now is injustice," Stevens says to Temple Drake. "Only truth can cope with that. Or love.").

But Faulkner loves and admires Stevens, and elects him to represent "the verities of the human heart" in their struggle against chaos and darkness. In *Requiem for a Nun,* Stevens has the line that may be the most quoted and most resonant in all the Faulkner canon: "The past is never dead. It's not even past."

In the gallery of archetypes, archvillains, rustics, and grotesques who populate Yoknapatawpha County, Stevens is the character in whom most of Faulkner's male readers choose to see themselves. A bachelor lawyer and intellectual, a judge's son descended of an old county family, Stevens is a graduate of Harvard and Heidelberg (of Germany, not Ohio) whose deepest passion—after Eula Varner Snopes and her daughter—is translating the Old Testament back into Greek.

Lawyer Stevens has his demons and his blind spots. But it's his role as the conscience of the community that establishes a moral center for the whole Yoknapatawpha cycle, and provides the model for characters like Atticus Finch in Harper Lee's *To Kill a Mockingbird.* Stevens often despairs of the townspeople—"the poor bastards" he calls them, Snopeses and all—but he never denies that he's one of them, blood of their blood. He never dreams of retreating from his responsibility.

Most of us from small towns, after reading Faulkner, looked around and tried to identify our own Gavin Stevens, our "bucolic Cincinnatus" in a rumpled flannel suit. Most of us were disappointed. Gavin Stevens is almost a wishful fantasy. He's the small town's answer to a comic-book superhero, a Batman or Superman watching over the sleeping citizens of Gotham or Metropolis. Faulkner's description of Stevens in *Requiem* would stir Bruce Wayne: "Champion not so much of truth as of justice, or of justice as he sees it, constantly involving himself, often for no pay, in affairs of equity and passion and even crime too among his people, white and Negro both."

Someone's watching, we need to think, even if God is far away. Gavin Stevens cares when no one else does. He can match wits, if not fists, with anyone. As County Attorney, he has tangible power to intervene when injustice is imminent. As the last knight of the old order, however, Stevens resembles Don Quixote more than Galahad. His antiquated chivalry often leads him into folly.

"What he was doing," explains his nephew Chick, after Stevens's disastrous assault on Eula Snopes's lover, "was simply defending forever with his blood the principle that chastity and virtue in women shall be defended whether they exist or not."

"You fool," his brother-in-law scolds him as Stevens bleeds into a basin. "Don't you know you can't fight? You don't know how."

And Stevens answers, "Can you suggest a better way to learn?"

But Faulkner's quixotic knight-errant is always more than a voyeur and a meddler, more than the nemesis of Snopeses and the self-appointed protector of women's honor. Murderers, rapists, lynch mobs, and the Ku Klux Klan test his mettle (though Faulkner dismisses the Klan in Yoknapatawpha County as a brief infatuation of Snopes-led ignoramuses). We see the Great War, where he serves in AFS ambulances behind Verdun, sober and temper Stevens and destroy his naive love affair with German idealism.

No two critics agree about the extent to which Stevens is Faulkner, or vice versa. But going back to the fiction, in the year of the author's centennial, we can see the literary hero as he saw Stevens—all too human, flawed, and vulnerable. No novelist was ever guilty of more metaphysical dithering and psychological nitpicking, no one ever tangled the strands of his plots more diabolically, like a perverse child playing with spaghetti. No one wasted more time pondering the imponderable role of heredity in the human drama.

Faulkner's miracle—besides his irresistible enthusiasm for his own creations—lies in his tender, almost sacramental compassion for the dumb brute in britches, "the poor son of a bitch," stumbling toward what he hopes is the light. ("The salvation of the world is in man's suffering, is that it?" asks Stevens.)

As his famous Nobel Prize speech emphasizes, Faulkner never gave up hope. His antique idealism was carved of granite. But I take his exaggerated fear of Snopeses to mean that he couldn't imagine moral authority prevailing outside the small-town matrix of history and family that could produce a Gavin Stevens.

I can't either. I can't imagine the Gavin Stevens of the strip mall, the subdivision, the formless suburban sprawl, the gated golf community. And what about the newest community, the "virtual" community of the Internet, church of the great god Gates? I detect no moral authority of any kind; and Snopeses proliferate in cyberspace, including some of the most depraved descendants of that modest pornographer Montgomery Ward, proprietor of "Atelier Monty."

Reliable moral leadership occurs only where the leader is inseparable from the fabric of the community—which first means there has to *be* a fabric. What would Faulkner have made of Bill Clinton, like Gavin Stevens a small-town Southern lawyer with a Cadillac education, who professes the highest ideals? (And like Wal-Mart, from Arkansas.) Is Clinton a Stevens, or a Snopes?

Percy Among the Nightingales

My friend Tim McLaurin—a native of the North Carolina sand-hills—once told his wife that her arguments for temperance were impressive enough, but he'd continue to drink because it was part of his heritage. This wistful appeal to principle, highly prejudicial to the future of his marriage, made a big impression on all of us. Could we legitimately claim the conspicuous consumption of alcoholic beverages as a tradition that sets Southerners apart? To what extent has it affected our literary heritage? No one disputes that William Faulkner and Thomas Wolfe were men of prodigious thirst—but no greater thirst than Midwesterners like F. Scott Fitzgerald, Ernest Hemingway, and Sinclair Lewis. Certainly the lives of Southern poets, past and present, have been governed in no small part by the volatile trinity of alcohol, eros, and narcissism. Yet the late James Dickey, whom most of us accepted as the gold standard for bibulous poets, humbly yielded the prize to Hart Crane (1899–1932), a Yankee poet and a gay one at that.

"I've always felt that I could drink with most men," Dickey wrote in *Sorties,* after reading Crane's biography. "But I could not stay with Hart Crane's alcoholic consumption for half an hour."

Drinking was never a regional vice, in America. When I hear men talk about their fathers, I'm convinced that the biggest untold story of the American century is the way alcoholic rituals set their stamp on generations of fathers and sons.

There remains a suspicion that the South is unique. The historian Henry Adams quotes an Englishman visiting Kentucky in 1800:

"They drink ardent spirits from morn till night . . . the truth is, their stomachs are depraved by burning liquors and they have no appetite for anything but what is highly flavored and strongly impregnated by salt." One Volney, a later English traveler, agrees: "To give tone to the wearied stomach, they drink Madeira, rum, French brandy, gin or malt spirits, which complete the ruin of their nervous systems."

Frederick Law Olmsted, a prominent Yankee touring the antebellum South in the 1850s, refers to "alcoholic liquor of the most fiery and pernicious description." But the Magna Carta of genteel substance abuse, the Declaration of Dependence that most eloquently defines a Southern drinker's heritage is Walker Percy's famous essay on bourbon published in *Esquire* in 1975. It's uncanny to me that so many men who drink and write have appropriated Percy's wry, urbane, mildly mournful tribute to "the aesthetic" of bourbon drinking for our private reserves of romantic rationalization. There's one passage we all quote or steal or read to each other:

> As between these evils and the aesthetic of Bourbon drinking, that is, the use of Bourbon to warm the heart, to reduce the anomie of the late 20th century, to cut the cold phlegm of Wednesday afternoons, I choose the aesthetic. What after all is the use of not having cancer, cirrhosis and such if a man comes home from work every day at five-thirty to the exurbs of Montclair or Memphis and there is the grass growing and the little family looking not quite at him but just past the side of his head, and there's Cronkite on the tube and the smell of pot roast in the living room, and inside the house and outside in the pretty exurb has settled the noxious particles and the sadness of the old dying Western world, and him thinking: "Jesus, is this it? Listening to Cronkite and the grass growing?"

For drinkers of a Southern persuasion, the image of this saturnine aristocrat cutting his cold phlegm with an amber tumbler of the South's own "milk of mercy" has become a kind of icon. We drink for our own reasons and most often alone, but Percy, by joining us, conferred a touch of class on the whole melancholy business. He was by blood and nurture a man of the Mississippi Delta, and *Homo mississippiensis*—white planter class, late twentieth century—was a creature for whom whiskey appears to have been an indispensable consolation.

"Quite simply, Percy liked to drink," biographer Jay Tolson admits in *Pilgrim in the Ruins*. "Percy's fondness for the bosky bite of bourbon neat fell just short of idolatry."

Tolson's is one of several excellent biographies published in the decade since Percy died. What bothers me is that each, to a greater or lesser degree, has portrayed Percy as a spiritual success story—the man whose Catholic faith carried him to the finish line, the rare artist who won his bets, conquered his demons, resolved his doubts, and bounded off to meet his Maker with a confident tread. In the same spirit, they interpret his novels more and more confidently as precise road maps for the Christian pilgrim, edifying parables for the pious in a tradition that goes back to John Bunyan and Dante Alighieri.

"Faith as a means of knowledge, as perhaps the highest form of knowledge, was the enabling condition of Percy's art," writes Jay Tolson. "The end of art was knowledge, which to Percy was knowledge of the Christian message."

I can't buy all of that. It makes Percy sound safe and smug. It's not a question of the Catholic party seizing him posthumously and putting their theological spin on his fiction. They can quote chapter and verse compellingly. Though he bridled against his designation as a "Southern" novelist, Percy repeatedly, defiantly declared himself a true believer with a Christian message. In his *Esquire* self-interview, Percy the author asks Percy the interviewer, "Do you mean do I believe the dogma the Catholic church proposes for belief?"

"Yes," responds the interviewer, and the author answers, "Yes."

"But how is that possible in this day and age?"

"What else is there?"

The scandal of Christianity, Percy called it. It gave him pleasure to invoke this scandal whenever he thought he was addressing the secular humanists and timid agnostics prevalent in literary and academic communities.

No one questions Percy's sincerity; no gentleman takes issue with another man's faith. But suppose the next generation of readers comes to Percy's work expecting some kind of literary Billy Graham, some happy warrior for Christ?

What kind of man was he, actually? There are people who have seen the light, and there are people who suspect that the light at the end of the tunnel is a runaway freight train. Most friends and associates of Walker Percy would have placed him among the trainspotters. He was a man of dark moods and self-destructive impulses, subject to what euphemists call "nervous illness." He was never at any safe distance from despair.

A black humorist Percy was, a writer of bitter, corrosive wit. His constant themes are loneliness and separateness—alienation served chilled, with a twist of irony. He was no reformer but a stoic who took the dimmest view of human progress.

"The present age is demented," he wrote shortly before his death. "It is possessed by a sense of dislocation, a loss of personal identity, an alternating sentimentality and rage which, in an individual patient, could be characterized as dementia."

When Percy was in his late fifties, and had been a Catholic for twenty-five years, he went through some debilitating crises of faith, including one period when he was unable to swallow the host during Holy Communion. He reverted at that stage to the consolations of bourbon, to the degree that his daughter Mary Pratt once admonished him, "You'll just have to crawl out of that bottle on your own."

"I'm told I am a mean low-down drunk, many sneers and insults to waiters etc.," Percy wrote to Shelby Foote.

Sober, Percy could be a bit of a crackpot, as any reader gleans from later books like *Lost in the Cosmos* and *The Thanatos Syndrome*. Nor should it be overlooked that he was incorrigibly sly, or that he described novelists as "a devious lot to begin with, disinclined to say anything straight out, especially about themselves, since their stock-in-trade is indirection." And he states clearly, in *Signposts*, "The novelist has no business setting up as the Answer Man."

We've hardly got a fair fight here for possession of Walker Percy—on one side a rabble of drinkers, malcontents, and melancholiacs, on the other a crack regiment of the soldiers of Christ. But Percy was an infinitely complex individual who published such a detailed map of his psyche. There ought to be enough of him to go around. I can't fault Catholic scholars for boasting about their distinguished and adamant convert. It only galls me when they seem to characterize Percy's fiction as a series of beguiling homilies he delivered with a vial of holy water behind his back. My guess is that he was holding a tumbler of one-hundred-proof Jack Daniel's.

Binx Bolling and Will Barrett were never, to me, characters who would be incomprehensible if we removed them from the shadow of the Cross. I'll argue that no first-rate fiction was ever written by anyone who was too certain about anything—and that includes salvation. By its nature serious literature is a search, a search informed by the knowledge that the search never ends.

It's not as if the bourbon party were scheming to snatch Percy's soul from Christian heaven and send it back to some boozy doubter's purgatory. If the Church could just reduce the odor of sanctity and allow the communion of saints to loan him, from time to time, back to the communion of sinners where he seemed so comfortable. The Church has so many eloquent defenders, and whiskey has so few.

"Bourbon does for me," Percy wrote, "what a piece of cake did for Proust."

Some of my best friends are Christians; I'm not out to provoke Catholics or substance abuse counselors either. The Christian faith is a clean and elegant solution to the anomie and the "sadness of the old dying Western world." Whiskey is a ragged, half-baked one. Yet whiskey is a solution—let's say a strategy—more accessible to most people of Walker Percy's neurotic temperament. Many spiritual, thoughtful people never achieve the kind of religious certainty Percy claimed for himself. They lack his will and his intellectual equipment, which was so well suited to beat reasonable doubt at its own exasperating game.

No major Southern writer ever swam so effortlessly in the deep waters of philosophical inquiry, or fought so hard to find his God. If such a wealth of intellect and spirit never freed Walker Percy from a certain reliance on whiskey—if drinking was a part of his heritage he continued to find useful, often irresistible—it's a fact we don't want to erase from the permanent record.

Which should it be, the official portrait—a mordant Percy drinking bourbon or a beatific Percy drinking communion wine? Why does it still matter to some of us? For my part, I never felt much affinity with the saved or the born again, Catholic or Protestant. I felt total sympathy with a writer like Percy who tested all the propositions and explored all the avenues relevant to faith or despair—and kept on drinking.

The Tennessee Stud

In a moment of discouragement, a writer I know calculated that every serious book aims itself at the same five hundred serious readers, an elite that doesn't necessarily include book reviewers. After twenty years on the circuit, he added, a writer has made the acquaintance of at least half of these serious readers. He sees their faces when he sits down to write.

Five hundred is a desperately small number; the word "serious" defies definition. But everyone knows what he means. In an adolescent culture that celebrates illiteracy, literature is once again an intimate enterprise. If publishing is a sprawling flea market of dubious merchandise, the serious business of writing and reading is transacted in one small tent at the edge of the field: Admission by password only. For years one of the passwords has been "Cormac McCarthy."

Thoughtful critics hail McCarthy as the foremost Southern writer of his generation, and even as the most gifted novelist writing in the English language. Yet before Knopf engineered the commercial success of his sixth novel *(All the Pretty Horses,* 1992)—in part by compelling him to submit to an interview with the *New York Times*—most English professors had never read McCarthy, and many had never heard of him. None of his first five novels sold more than five thousand copies in hardback. Without too much effort he could have located all his readers and mailed them questionnaires.

We never heard from him. McCarthy's reclusiveness and disdain for self-promotion guaranteed his obscurity but enhanced the mystique of a hermit genius. Not even the praise of his peers could smoke him

out of hiding. Nominated for a charter membership in the Fellowship of Southern Writers—by no less a champion than Walker
Percy—McCarthy respectfully declined. No other writer has refused
election to the Fellowship. McCarthy's rootlessness was another eccentricity that fed his legend. Few journalists or photographers pur-
sued him, but the ones who tried found a cold trail of budget ac-
commodations that led from Knoxville to Chicago, New Orleans,
Las Vegas, London, Paris, and El Paso. In one of the many books of
photographs of Southern writers—most of them posed for effect like
dust-jacket portraits—McCarthy is framed in the ticket window of an
abandoned train station, wearing an expression that combines an-
noyance and profound pity for a world where people might covet his
likeness.

"A cult following" is the cliché that perfectly describes McCarthy's
readership prior to *All the Pretty Horses.* But it was always the prose,
not the myth, that kept us in church. What is it about Cormac Mc-
Carthy, the philistines rage, that inspires such devotion? I'd argue
that there are only three things, none of them uncommon, that might
keep you from admiring McCarthy: a tin ear, a weak stomach, or a
hopeful heart.

If it's solace you're seeking, stay away. ("I know all souls are one
soul," says McCarthy's Cornelius Suttree, "and all souls lonely.") But
McCarthy at his best—McCarthy writing with the throttle wide
open—is still the closest thing to heroin you can buy in a bookstore.
Vereen Bell, who published the first book-length assessment of these
novels *(The Achievement of Cormac McCarthy,* 1988), acknowledges
McCarthy's incomparable style: "His language brings the real world
back to us replenished but still familiar, as if we were seeing it truly for
the first time."

My story with Cormac McCarthy is the story of a devout reader
and a writer he reveres. Idolatry was never a weakness of mine. Only
one encounter with a legend ever left me at a loss for words, and that
was in front of the visitor's dugout at Shea Stadium when I turned
suddenly to find Willie Mays grinning at me and holding out
his hand.

I was only twenty-five then. When I was pushing fifty, Cormac McCarthy produced a similar social dysfunction. I hope it doesn't embarrass Clyde Edgerton, a fair novelist himself, if I describe our behavior when McCarthy, wearing his name tag, materialized improbably at a cocktail party in Cashiers, North Carolina. Clyde and I sort of backed ourselves within earshot of his conversation, like awed undergraduates at a book signing. I'm not sure we'd have introduced ourselves at all if McCarthy hadn't turned and offered his hand, like Willie Mays.

"How do you like where you're living?" somebody asked him, and he answered, "I never liked anyplace much." I ended up eating a couple of meals with McCarthy, consciously trying to square this small, neat, courteous man in the blue seersucker jacket with the author of *Blood Meridian* and *Child of God.* There was no clue that I was passing the marmalade to a writer whose novels encompass necrophilia, incest, infanticide, and sex with consenting fruit. There's nothing physically remarkable about McCarthy either, except eyes of the lightest blue in the human spectrum—desert prophet eyes like Peter O'Toole's in *Lawrence of Arabia.* Eyes you don't want to play poker against, because they give away nothing at all.

We talked about our grandfathers. I was surprised to discover that McCarthy is a passionate golfer. The bond between a writer and his reader is a one-way illusion, one that personal contact never strengthens and sometimes destroys. I'm not sure we're ever intended to see the wizard behind the curtain. Try to imagine a game of golf with Tolstoi or Joyce.

Put me down as an eccentric footnote in the history of American literature, a man who turned down his chance to play golf with Cormac McCarthy. As an anecdote, I decided, it wasn't worth a threat to my hero-worship or the embarrassment of my long-abandoned golf game.

We all liked McCarthy, a pleasant man who shows no signs of the self-involvement and rogue-elephant willfulness common to artists who are praised above their fellows. My positive impression makes it more difficult for me to confess my misgivings about his border trilogy, which began with *All the Pretty Horses* and concluded with *Cities of the Plain.* But what does a reader owe a favorite writer, to whom he's offered wholehearted allegiance? Honesty, I think—not the craven rationalizations of the academic who yokes his career to certain writers and their reputations.

Who but your loyal readers will tell you the truth? I think Mc-Carthy, who left his native Appalachians for good with *Blood Meridian* (1985), has been seduced and in some way misled by the desert Southwest. I hope it's true that he's at last found a home, out where the antelope roam. No doubt the vanishing American cowboy is a wholesome obsession, compared with the pitiful outcasts and damaged, peripheral creatures who populate his earlier novels.

But the West can fool you, I think. I've been known to rhapsodize about Western skies and horses grazing against a backdrop of snow-capped ranges, and I own a Stetson the size of a wading pool. The West is expansive and spiritual, but it's physically empty in a way that entices you to add your own depth and meanings. Magic plants grow in the desert, plants that make you see things that aren't really there.

McCarthy might have heeded a warning from the late Wallace Stegner: "The West does not need to explore its myths much further; it has already relied on them too long." *The Crossing* (1994), the second book of the border trilogy, begins with a pure masterpiece of a novella about a boy and a wolf. The rest of the novel owes too much to Carlos Castaneda (I pray McCarthy wouldn't take that as a kick in the stomach). Castaneda's Don Juan, the Yaqui *brujo,* was the original model for these desert sages, gypsies, and blind philosophers, scarcely distinguishable from one another, who offer cryptic parables that tease us toward the meaning of life.

"Oracular" is an unbecoming mode for fiction. When Flaubert said that a great writer should stand in his novel "like God in his Creation, everywhere and yet invisible," he didn't mean disguised as omniscient pilgrims and mysterious hitchhikers.

Cities of the Plain (1998) is a fine tragic novel, better than most of us could write in a lifetime of grim commitment. But it's Western mythology with all its buckskin trim, with a nod to Larry McMurtry. In place of cursed pariahs, we find upright, compassionate characters who might have borrowed their values from "Gene Autry's Ten Cowboy Commandments." Evil trumps virtue, as it always does in McCarthy's novels. But a Mexican pimp with a wicked switchblade is a pale successor to *Blood Meridian*'s terrifying Judge Holden, who outdeviled Satan himself. And McCarthy the oracle is at it again in *Cities of the Plain,* most unhappily in an epilogue choked with perishable profundity.

A century from now, if the habit of literature survives the current cultural holocaust, *Suttree* will be a benchmark of literacy like *Huckleberry Finn* or *The Sound and the Fury.* It pains me to see *Suttree*'s author chided by some lightweight New York reviewer for "portentous rhetoric" and "pop existentialism." But McCarthy has been asking for it. He should pay a visit home to Tennessee, where stoic cowboys and desert oracles don't much signify, where even the best readers resent untranslated Spanish dialogue.

His material success is richly deserved and long overdue. Even outcasts have the right to grow old in comfort. But McCarthy's old readers liked him standing out there on a ridge in the thunder and lightning, expounding (in the words of Vereen Bell) on "the true horror of death, the impersonal relentlessness of time, the cruel absence of God from the world." We wish he'd throw us raw meat, like he used to.

Burying a False Witness

> Darling Jill felt the returning surge of savage excitement grip her. . . . She stood it as long as she could, and then she ran and fell at his feet, hugging his knees and kissing him all over. Will laid his hands on her head and stroked her hair.
>
> She stirred jerkily, rising to her knees and thrusting her body between his legs, and locked her arms around his waist. Her head was buried against him, and she hugged him with her arms and shoulders. It was only when she could find his hands that she lay still against him. One after the other she kissed his fingers, pushing them between her lips and into her mouth. But after that, she was still not satisfied.
>
> . . . "What time is it?" he asked after a while.
>
> —*God's Little Acre*

Today this is soft-core porn; you find it in women's magazines. When Erskine Caldwell published it, in 1933, it was hot enough to scorch his dust jacket and render critics wide-eyed and weak-kneed from Tobacco Road to Times Square. Will is neither husband nor lover to Darling Jill, you understand—he's her brother-in-law, and across the room his wife (her sister) sits calmly in a rocking chair during the entire performance.

The adoration of Will Thompson is a set piece only Caldwell would have attempted. Will, a cotton-mill worker, symbolizes the working-class superman, like those giants with sledgehammers on Soviet propaganda posters. He's about to be martyred heroically in an uprising against the mill bosses. The sexual force field of such a colossal manhood is so powerful that no woman could deny her sister's need to enter it. On the previous page, Will has invoked his proletarian divine right to rape another sister-in-law, the exquisite Griselda, whose sexual aura is as irresistible as his own.

It's entertaining to imagine how Will Thompson would go over with contemporary critics, who replace class struggles with gender wars and purge the canon of all its testosterone titans. The deconstruction of *God's Little Acre* is a performance I'd pay hard cash to witness from a ringside seat. A favorite concept in the academy of the '90s was "the frailty of the author." If you follow these things, you know this means that a writer is merely a conduit for the prevailing ideas and attitudes of one race, gender, and social class at one moment in history. To the strictest postmodern critic, an author is something like a helpless pointer on the Ouija board of literature.

Erskine Caldwell confounds them. He was a rogue wave, a one-man literary movement. God knows he was frail, by any moral or intellectual yardstick. But no critic anywhere could demonstrate that "texts" like *God's Little Acre* were just what we might expect, in the depths of the Great Depression, from this East Georgia preacher's son. That they were compared in their day to the fiction of Twain, Faulkner, and Balzac, that Caldwell was hailed as a genius by Malcolm Cowley, Lewis Mumford, Jean-Paul Sartre, and Albert Camus—these things may never be adequately explained. What Caldwell and his once-exalted reputation illustrate most convincingly is the chronic frailty of the *critic*.

Before he turned thirty, Caldwell had achieved not only international notoriety but a nearly unprecedented level of critical recognition. He was championed by Ezra Pound and H. L. Mencken. As late as 1960 he was under serious consideration for the Nobel Prize. Saul Bellow, for one, believed that he should have had it. To Brooks Atkinson, dean of American drama critics, Caldwell was "a demonic genius—brutal, grimly comic and clairvoyant."

When Caldwell died in 1987, at eighty-three, Dartmouth College opened its collection of his papers to researchers. Several biographies resulted, but Dan Miller's from Knopf was the first released by a major publisher. It's well worth reading—not because Caldwell deserves resurrection, but because there's no case study anywhere that sheds more light on the perverse way literary reputations are made and unmade in America.

To understand how completely Erskine Caldwell has vanished from the literary firmament, all we need is Dan Miller's confession that he was twenty-seven when he first heard the writer's name. That seems incredible to some of us a generation older, to whom Erskine Caldwell was a name as familiar as Joe Louis, Harry Truman, or Arthur Godfrey. When he hit his second peak in the early '50s, Caldwell had already sold a world-record 55 million books in hardcover and paperback editions (now seventy million-plus). The paperbacks with their sordid, suggestive cover art—leering rednecks touching the crotches of their overalls, swooning farm girls with huge breasts spilling out of ragged blouses—were a part of every private library. Often they were the most private part, slipped under mattresses and concealed under stacks of *Saturday Evening Posts* where the kids wouldn't find them, though we always did.

From the movie version of *God's Little Acre* (1957) we took away an indelible image of Tina Louise as the incomparable Griselda. Grim decades of *Gilligan's Island*—Tina played Ginger—never entirely erased her erotic mystique. But these are old men's memories. Dan Miller, a Harvard Ph.D. candidate when he discovered Erskine Caldwell, wasn't even born when Tina's "rising beauties" briefly eclipsed Marilyn Monroe's.

The scholar's gold mine that drew Miller to Dartmouth turned out to be a fairly nasty old landfill. What Miller's research reveals about Caldwell is almost uniformly disturbing. The writer was cruel, hypocritical, conniving, greedy, self-absorbed to the point of obtuseness, a man of few friends who betrayed the few he had.

He was a possessive, manipulative, abusive husband to at least three of his four wives. He beat, terrified, and neglected his children. He became a sad and sloppy drunk. His lone moral asset, a gift from his father, was a well-developed social conscience for his time and place. But his passion for the underdog, black or white, evolved into a lucrative industry for Caldwell and the source of some of the dreariest, most predictable fiction in all the bleeding-heart canon.

The key to Caldwell's net worth as an interpreter of our times probably lies in his repeated declaration that he was "a writer, not a reader." It happens that I've heard this strange boast from several writers. One, who need not be named here, has also been touted for the Nobel Prize. A couple of others were idiots who would soon return to busing tables. A writer who boasts that he doesn't read is like a fish who boasts that he doesn't need water. It won't be long before we're holding our noses.

Since Caldwell described himself as a nonreader, and since his fiction putrefied in a manner consistent with total intellectual isolation, we don't need to exhume his library card to prove that he was one of these poor fish. James Baldwin, a critic who wasn't taken in by Caldwell's reputation or his radical credentials, declared him dead as a writer in 1947, when Caldwell was forty-four. "Unless we hear from him again in accents more individual," Baldwin wrote, "we can leave his bones for that literary historian of another day."

Dan Miller makes the most of these old bones, acknowledging that the dogs have buried them in some places you'd hate to dig. By 1960 Caldwell was a bitter hack reduced to selling stories to slick T&A magazines like *Playboy, Cavalier, Swank,* and *Gent.* Miller deals honestly with Caldwell's sorry character and the pitiful quality of most of his fiction. But he shies away from the great mystery of Caldwell's reputation. With a humility altogether fitting in a biographer so young, Miller declines to challenge the literary lions of the '30s who welcomed Erskine Caldwell to their pride. He generously decides that there must have been magic in the early novels that somehow vanished from all the rest.

I'm too old to be so humble. Though Caldwell published twenty novels and more than a hundred stories, his critical reputation rested largely on the merits of *Tobacco Road* (1932) and *God's Little Acre*

(1933). Miller's book compels us to read or reread them. They're quick reads, especially *God's Little Acre*. They will astonish you. If they impress you, then you and I operate on different aesthetic assumptions.

They're literary Frankensteins, of crude materials crudely stitched together. Jonathan Daniels of the Raleigh newspaper clan hailed *God's Little Acre* as "one of the finest studies of the Southern poor white which has ever come into our literature," which must be one of the most obtuse critical assessments ever rendered in print. It raises the possibility that Daniels, from a family with a notably low incidence of pellagra, had never encountered a Southern poor white face to face.

Dan Miller documents conclusively that Caldwell, born and raised in rural Georgia, the son of a well-educated but often indigent Presbyterian minister, encountered any number of poor whites. That seems to indict him more hopelessly, because the characters in his novels are the same grotesque stereotypes immortalized on hillbilly postcards. They teach us as much about poor whites as the minstrel shows taught us about black people. And subsequent experience— the hookworm belt became his "beat" as a well-paid left-wing journalist—never seemed to deepen or sharpen Caldwell's perceptions.

Ignorant of the fact that lust is one of the first casualties of extreme hunger, he created starving subhuman characters and endowed them with rampaging superhuman libidos. Caldwell's sharecroppers sniff and rub and lick and mount each other as unselfconsciously as rutting dogs or lab rats. But like the worst of Henry Miller it's all phallic fantasy, projections of the author's personal pathology. It's well documented that the preacher's son had a thunderous sexual awakening. According to his first wife, Helen Lannigan, he disarmed her with the seductive proposition, "I'd like to knock you on the head with a rock and fuck you."

Miller reports that the young Caldwell was fascinated with "the obscene." It's a cruel thing to say, but some of his novels are so misbegotten I wonder if perpetual tumescence diverted a critical supply of blood from Caldwell's brain. Though sex was his obsession, he was no Rabelais. Even in the permissive '90s, "disgusting" is the only word for the infamous turnip scene that kept the Broadway version of *Tobacco Road* running for eight years.

How did the critical establishment of the '30s mistake this coarse stuff for literature? They weren't entirely blind. Above all Caldwell was a crank, an odd duck. His radical admirers, like Mike Gold of *The Masses,* knew there was something queer about him—the way he tossed farce and tragedy together as if he couldn't tell the difference, as if he knew a bold recipe for fiction no one else had attempted.

They questioned his strange shifts of tone and chided him for his superficial grasp of politics. But they never questioned his integrity as a witness. Caldwell's South, a land of terrified Negroes and degraded sharecroppers starved by heartless capitalists and landowners, was precisely the one required by the Marxist worldview. The popular Marxist subtheme of sexual liberation didn't hurt Caldwell either.

My guess is that New York radicals knew as much about Georgia as they knew about Suriname, and like ancient cartographers were only too ready to populate the unknown regions with fabulous monsters. Caldwell was a fellow-traveling native of the region who offered monsters to spare. Of course there was never anyone in Georgia like Ty Ty or Darling Jill. There were *worse*—inbred, pellagra-hollowed Kallikaks shortchanged by the economy and the gene pool—but the gregarious, philosophical Ty Ty Walden would sound like a New York actor to the likes of them.

It was the Bolshevik PC of the day that made a prophet of this palpably flawed and unreliable witness. But it created a man without a country. Caldwell was spoiled and misled by the Northern Left and disowned by most Southerners, who naturally hated to see themselves portrayed fornicating like rabbits on crack. He left the South when he was twenty-seven and never really returned, cutting himself off from any source of inspiration that might have compensated for his lack of intellectual curiosity.

The gullibility of those radical critics raised up a myopic giant with feet of red clay. It also legitimized stereotypes that plague the South to this day. There should be a lesson in humility here for academic critics who threaten to take over literature entirely and put those frail authors out to pasture. Here's a proposition I think I can prove: No first-rate writer was ever half as blinkered by tribal conventions, or by intellectual fads and fashions, as his average critical adversary.

Erskine Caldwell's precipitous fall doesn't seem as cruel if we acknowledge, as I do, that his rise was a big mistake. His vision of the South may be no more misleading or dishonest than the visions of Margaret Mitchell, the Fugitives, "the Richmond-Charleston School," or any of the other romanticizers and apologists Caldwell so detested. But it was a crackpot, sometimes almost lunatic vision, elevated by frail critics to a most improbable authority. It devolved into a dismal, unvarying formula.

Dan Miller did us all a great service when he reopened this dusty old file. Now it's time to close it. Many Southerners said all along that Erskine Caldwell was the joint creation of dumb Yankee critics and smart Yankee businessmen, who made a mountain out of a dunghill. Time has eroded that unsavory mountain in a very appropriate fashion.

A Cobbler's Petition

When the news is unbearable I like to spend an hour rummaging through the family archives, of which I have become the principal keeper. There's an anodyne effect from fading letters in antique script, commencement programs, wedding invitations, newspaper obituaries worn tissue-thin, marbled photographs of turn-of-the-century cousins whose names will never be retrieved; a yearbook dedicated to Miss Lillian Achilles (true), school librarian, a maiden lady with a pince-nez, wrapped in fur, her black voile dress gathered above her bosom with a cameo head of Athena.

The most surprising thing I ever found, I found in a high-school literary magazine dated 1930: an eight-line poem, unrhymed, attributed to my father. Poems, to the best of my knowledge, had never been his style. I won't subject him to the cruel scrutiny of modern critics by reproducing those verses. His inspiration was autumn leaves, an invitation to the obvious then and now. He was sixteen, after all.

But in the concluding lines he apologizes for distractions that blinded him to beauty:

> I reveled through in uglier sights
> Machines and noisy man-made things.
> That now in weariness I flee.

The revelation was that it sounded exactly like me, and nothing like my father. He loved cars and clothes, big bands, big productions. I'm the born Luddite, anchorite, forest hermit, destroyer of telephones. When was he weary? But the poem connected me with a piece of my father that opened him up to reinterpretation, more than any of his lectures or the few letters he wrote, more than his diaries, which I have. It made me feel more securely that I was his son.

I mean psychologically, Mom. Every poet is obliged to shed his everyday voice, trained to hide things, and find that other voice that gives things away—not always the same things the poet set out to give away. Even the most mannered, conventional verse may shed more light on its author than a dozen earnest letters to the editor. An honest poet, with or without great skill, is like a house with no curtains.

People can see in, if they bother to look. And that, at most times in most communities, is considered bad form. Never worse than now. Poet Dave Smith, editor of the *Southern Review*, claims that poetry's "lyrical effusion" is an embarrassment to the stage managers of Southern literature ("SoLitCrit doesn't like art personal, effused") and accounts for its exclusion from the inner circle.

Emotional exhibitionism has become a cultural misdemeanor, while educated readers root through haystacks of minimalist text for needles of insight. The decline of poetry, like the decline of language itself, has been well documented. I was one of the few to lodge a protest when the *Los Angeles Times* and the *Washington Post* banished poetry reviews from their book pages. A street-corner survey showed that the average American is unable to name a single living poet; half of the subjects thought Shakespeare wrote novels, and a significant minority thought Chaucer was an early astronomer; the one who claimed to know Robert Penn Warren identified him as the Chief Justice.

When newspaper prose aspires to television and both of them pay homage to the *National Enquirer,* the language of poets recedes rapidly in the rearview mirror. As they lost readers on the high side and on the low, poets huddled together for survival, holed up in universities and writers' colonies, published in small magazines and small presses that Waldenbooks doesn't carry. Their work naturally took a turn toward opacity and solipsism, and little of it filtered out.

In the absence of poets, prose rules carelessly. As readers in the mainstream, we lose the habit of poetry. One of my Christmas gifts from my wife was a collection of poems *(The Transparent Man,* 1990) by Anthony Hecht, who has been my single favorite poet ever since James Dickey, in person, scared the daylights out of me in New York in 1969.

It was Hecht's first book in a decade, and I opened it with something close to erotic anticipation. But I wasn't ready. Dulled by that rank Ganges of literal-minded prose, the "news" that helps me to make a living, I'd lost not only the habit of serious attention but even the habit of play. Here in "Curriculum Vitae," the first poem, what does he mean that children in winter "manufacture ghosts"? I grope around for some psychological handle and then thump my empty head in humiliation: He means their breath freezing, in clouds above their heads. And "ferned and parslied windows," which I stumbled over without comprehension, that's just frost on the window.

Our capacity for language shrinks rapidly if we don't exercise it, and poetry is the only exercise that engages every muscle group. Hecht is a true poet, and a true poet's words take up more space than any other words—more space on the page, in the memory, even in that limpid millpond of the air that the bard may set to rippling with his shouts.

In the best poetry the words are breathing, like Hecht's children, and they manufacture ghosts and pictures. Real poetry is luminous and numinous, but best of all it's precise. In the best hands, its precision is awesome. Novelists release floods of words and then go back over them like inspectors on an assembly line, looking for defects and duds. Journalists choose their words as carefully as they can, under the circumstances, under the clock. But a gifted poet in his pride will never release a word he's ashamed of, and his best choices can cut like a laser.

There's an essay by Dave Smith that asserts the superiority of poetic expression, and then pulls the trigger: "The rest [of literature] is mostly information *cobbled* together" (my italics). *Cobbled.* Can you see us poor prose monkeys there in the dim light, hunched over our little benches with our little hammers, working stiff leather with stiff fingers? *Cobbled.* It's a choice so devastatingly correct there's no rejoinder, no defense. After that verb, the room falls silent. The poet has spoken.

Or take "Common Form," from *Epitaphs of the War* published by Rudyard Kipling in 1919, when poets were still public men and the last war of all had just been fought: "If any question why we died, / Tell them, because our fathers lied."

Poets have every right to their arrogance, to their wounded tribal pride. They have been neglected, quarantined, reduced to an audience of "mostly magnolia maidens and academics," according to Smith. But the rumors that alarm me are the rumors of separatism, of deliberate secession during the verbal collapse of a waning civilization. It's nothing new, this conviction that poets should write only for other poets. Robert Graves and his lover Laura Riding shared it passionately, seventy years ago.

"True poets will agree," Graves sneered, "that poetry is spiritual illumination delivered by a poet to his equals, not an ingenious technique of swaying a popular audience or of enlivening a sottish dinner party."

Curse you, man. To me this sounds like desertion under fire. Who ever finds the audience that he thinks he deserves? The language is slipping away from precision, toward manipulation and concealment, vulgarity and chaos. When we lose our precision we lose meanings; when we lose enough meanings we lose our perspective, and our sanity. We fight wars and talk gibberish to defend them. The hour is late.

Call this a cobbler's petition, to poets who may be sulking in their tents. Don't abandon us, don't give us up. Sometimes your erudition is too much. Even if we had the learning for it once, few of us have maintained it. We haven't kept up. But we're still listening, still counting on you. The plague is spreading fast, and what becomes of us if the last few physicians will only treat each other?

The Paris of the South

I'll never write another line
for anything but love
in this city where steam
rises off the street after
a rain like bosoms heaving.
—Everette Maddox, "New Orleans"

NEW ORLEANS

An invasion by 28,000 bibliophiles is no rival to Mardi Gras, in this self-absorbed city that hasn't lost its composure since Andy Jackson's cannon bid the British farewell in 1815. But concurrent conventions of the American Library Association and the Friends of the Library kept the restaurants full and the bookstores swarming. The notorious service at the Cafe du Monde slowed to an escargot's pace; librarians consumed entire paperbacks waiting for beignets.

The library congress compared very favorably to the Republican Convention I covered here in 1988, when bookstores stood empty and escort services worked double shifts. The book people shifted the tourist focus from Bourbon Street to places like the Faulkner House in Pirates Alley, behind the cathedral. In this old Creole townhouse where William Faulkner dwelt briefly in 1925, Joe Di Salvo and Rosemary James sell rare books, first editions, and serious literature to a discriminating clientele.

It's a place where you might meet Cormac McCarthy, the hermit genius of Southern letters, who recently dropped in to browse. At the Faulkner House you can book a literary walking tour of the French Quarter with Kenneth Holditch, a University of New Orleans professor who was a member of Walker Percy's famous writing class at Loyola.

Literary history? The Quarter's might be richer, per square foot, than anything south of Greenwich Village. A few blocks between Jackson Square and Canal Street contain sites sacred to forty or fifty writers whose work has survived, in an unbroken line from Lafcadio Hearn to Truman Capote. Holditch, a bearded, dapper individual of indeterminate age, knew many of them personally. As he recounted their stories, we crowded into the meager shade of a palm tree in Jackson Square and watched big stained thunderheads roll up the river from the Gulf.

A few of these writers were born in New Orleans. Most of them came here to escape something. It was the same thing, usually—the heavy weight of small-town, middle-class, Bible Belt families and their orderly expectations. A more affluent class of artists and dreamers went off to Paris. But New Orleans was the poor man's Paris, the Paris of the South. In the South but not of it. Walker Percy described New Orleans as "in a real sense adrift not only from the South but from the rest of Louisiana, somewhat like Mont Saint-Michel awash at high tide."

I came down here myself in 1967, in full flight from the Terrible Trinity of marriage, gainful employment, and the Selective Service. Though I stayed almost as long as Faulkner—six months—I can't remember writing anything besides the obscene limerick that won an English department competition at Loyola ("A clap-ridden emu named Bruce . . . ").

I lived with a professional football player and a Boston Irishman named Jimmy, the owner of the first private handgun I ever saw, who claimed that he was wanted for homicide in Massachusetts. We were fools, fairly wild by some people's reckoning. The Big Easy seemed to forgive us. William Faulkner, twenty-eight years old, used to sit up in his garret with a peashooter and sting priests and nuns with BB shot. In the game he played with his roommate, a clean hit on a black nun fetched the highest score.

That's one of Dr. Holditch's favorite stories. It made me think about this academic fascination with writer's lives. Generic immature behavior becomes precious literary anecdote if and when the writer achieves a reputation. We were visiting New Orleans on what they call a "book tour," to promote the paperback edition of my wife's most recent novel. Half the people we ate and drank with were published writers. No one did anything very colorful—it was an older crowd—but if one of those writers becomes the Faulkner or the Cormac McCarthy of the twenty-first century, will every stupid thing we said to each other turn up in someone's dissertation?

But there was a harder side to the Bohemian life of the Quarter. The stifling garret where Faulkner took aim at the nuns has no proper windows or ventilation, only an iron grate in the wall. It looks like a place where a runaway slave might be secretly quartered. At twenty-eight Faulkner had no money, no reputation, no publisher. At thirty-one, two years before the success of *The Glass Menagerie,* Tennessee Williams was in New Orleans waiting on tables and ushering at a movie theater.

The Quarter with its plaques and tour sites is like an old battlefield where great sacrifices were made for literature. Not all the city's starving artists went on to better things. Some went on to things that were much, much worse.

John Kennedy Toole, who wrote *A Confederacy of Dunces,* was thirty-two when he committed suicide. His novel was published posthumously. A great favorite among the younger generation of New Orleans writers was the poet Everette Maddox, who died in 1989 of cancer and extreme alcoholic deterioration. Maddox, who was forty-four, had been homeless for the last five years of his life. Like Faulkner, Maddox came to New Orleans from a small Southern town in the vast, vague countryside Creoles think of as "Upriver," to avail himself of the Crescent City's fabled freedoms and its sweet compliant muse.

Maddox wrote drunken love poems to elusive "Suzy," who may never have kissed him. But the muse kissed him on occasion. In *American Waste,* a collection published posthumously by his friends, I found this:

> And my Mother died of the late 20th Century
> where heaven was a hospital
> Well
> sleep well sweetheart
> over there
> on that hillside
> in Alabama
> by the railroad tracks
> in that long dress—
> you ain't missin' nothin'.

II

THE SWORD

In Stonewall's Shadow

In Stonewall's Shadow

On the scaffold in Charles Town, just before the hangman dropped the white hood over his head, John Brown turned to the sheriff and praised the view of the Shenandoah Valley:

"This is a beautiful country," said Brown. "I never truly had the pleasure of seeing it before."

"None like it," the sheriff replied.

It's a conversation several eyewitnesses recorded. Two other eyewitnesses, that chilly December morning in 1859, were Major Thomas Jonathan Jackson of the Virginia Military Institute—known to history as "Stonewall" but to his cadets as "Tom Fool"—and Private John Wilkes Booth of the Richmond militia. Biographers pass along the story from cadets in his detachment that Major Jackson had spent the night in fervent prayer for John Brown's soul. They were two of a kind, Brown and Jackson, fearless Christians who put their fate in God's hands; no individual was of any account, no action was harsh or excessive if God's greater glory was the goal. More than a few contemporaries thought both of them were crazy.

Not present at the hanging was the commanding officer of the company of marines who captured John Brown and recovered the federal arsenal at Harper's Ferry from Brown's abolitionist guerrillas. He was Lieutenant Colonel Robert E. Lee of the Second United States Cavalry, on home leave from his regiment in Texas.

Virginians are often reproached for smugness. ("I like Virginia and I like Virginians," William Faulkner said when he taught at the University of Virginia. "Because Virginians are all snobs and I like snobs.

A snob has to spend so much time being a snob that he has little left to meddle with you, and so it's very pleasant here.") But when they argue that God made Virginia as a special favor to the human race—and especially when they argue that no American history worth mentioning took place outside its borders—there's little to gain by disputing them.

My wife and I were back in the Shenandoah teaching some writing classes at Mary Baldwin College, in Staunton. Mary Baldwin, a women's college of antebellum origins, sits high on a hill, higher far than John Brown's scaffold. The landscape that stirred the old man, even as he stood at heaven's gate, is scarcely diminished by 140 years of progress. But even more striking, when you've been away, is the way this expansive landscape is cramped and crowded by the past.

Up here, history's like a madman (Staunton is the site of the state's oldest insane asylum) who stalks the streets shouting out famous names and dates, battle cries and patriotic speeches. At our inn we met a woman from Florida who was trying to see all of Virginia in one week. In four or five day trips, including digressions to wineries and craft shops, this pilgrim managed Appomattox Courthouse, Monticello and Mr. Jefferson's university, five or six Civil War battlefields, and the tombs and relics of Robert E. Lee and Stonewall Jackson at Lexington. She ventured as far as Richmond, and schemed to add Manassas, Williamsburg, and Mount Vernon if the weather held.

Within an easy morning's drive from Jefferson's aerie at Charlottesville are sites consecrated to every Virginia legend from Pocahontas to Stonewall's warhorse Sorrel, who outlived the general by twenty-three years and now stands preserved by the taxidermist's art in the Jackson museum at VMI. Directly across the street from our inn was the birthplace and memorial museum of Staunton's own Woodrow Wilson, the last (1856) of eight American presidents born in the state of Virginia.

Grant Massachusetts Plymouth Rock and Bunker Hill, Pennsylvania Independence Hall and Gettysburg. They can't protest when Virginia proclaims herself the Cradle of America. The Jamestown colony was the beginning. Washington and Jefferson created the Republic; Virginia's second wave of heroes fractured it or tempered and refined it, according to your view of the Civil War.

The Confederates still dominate the Shenandoah. A visitor from a more evolved, amnesiac and mongrelized part of the South cannot ignore a certain martial air—a military presence, as if the proud losers who fell short in 1863 have been quietly preparing, ever since, for the possibility of another chance to show their mettle.

VMI in Lexington, where the generals are buried, has been the South's last bastion (with The Citadel) of mostly white, all-male military education. Under relentless official pressure, VMI finally matriculated its first coed cadets in September 1997. Four of the thirty women had resigned before Thanksgiving, exhausted or appalled by the Rat Line, the Institute's infamous six-month ordeal of initiation.

But that freshman class lost forty-two males, as well. The military life is a hard sell to teenagers of the '90s, who no longer submit to marching orders from their parents. The famous Staunton Military Academy for boys was closed twenty years ago, and its buildings incorporated into Mary Baldwin College. Also defunct is Augusta Military Academy, just up the Valley from Staunton. It stands empty and eerie, tall gothic windows framing vacancy, just as VMI stood empty in 1861 when Major Jackson dismissed his cadets and sent them off to serve in the Army of Northern Virginia.

Yet the Old Guard fights on. Before VMI was compelled to admit women, the school developed a scheme to run a separate-but-equal corps of female cadets at Mary Baldwin. This experiment remains as the Virginia Women's Institute for Leadership, and its straight-spined recruits in starched ROTC uniforms double-time past slouching civilians.

No, Virginia, this is not the Seven Sisters. Anywhere on the Mary Baldwin campus, you take your bearings from the towering neon-edged sign of the Stonewall Jackson Hotel, a constant reminder that There Was Once A War. Here in the Valley it takes a forced march to escape Stonewall. A sign identifies one road as the Stonewall Jackson

Highway, the next one as the Lee-Jackson Highway. Just outside
Staunton are the battlefields of Cross Keys and Port Republic, text-
book victories in the Valley Campaign that made Jackson's reputation as a military tactician.

The War Between the States, never absent in the Valley, reemerged
in the mass media with the commercial and critical success of the
novel *Cold Mountain,* by North Carolina's Charles Frazier. *Cold
Mountain* is bringing more tourists and war buffs to Virginia. A few
of them, like me, will brood over the marble statues and stuffed
warhorses and wonder what the generals in gray would think of us—
what they'd think of the South, if they could view it now from a place
as high and lonely as John Brown's scaffold.

What they wrought, in their pride, was so dreadful. Most of the
dignity and glamour of that war—or any war—is manufactured by
schoolbook historians, for the express purpose of inducing future
generations of young men to enlist or submit to conscription. First-
hand accounts are uniformly terrifying, ghastly enough to dry up recruiting forever; but most young men, in any time or place, are not
avid readers.

"It's fortunate that war is so terrible," General Lee is supposed to
have said, "or else we should love it too much." But this ambivalence
seems limited to the generals. Enlisted men write of starvation and
sickness, random slaughter, rotting corpses, and satanic desolation.

"Their last hope had set," wrote Private Sam Watkins of the Tennessee men who served under General Braxton Bragg. "They hated
war. To their mind the South was a great tyrant, and the Confederacy
a fraud. They were deserting by the thousands."

In his memoir, *Co. Aytch,* Watkins lingers over the shooting, flog-
ging, and branding—on both hips, with a cattle iron—of wretched
deserters by General Bragg: "A merciless tyrant . . . he loved to crush
the spirit of his men. Not a single soldier in the whole army ever
loved or respected him."

Twenty thousand of these reluctant rebels fell at Gettysburg, and
many of their generals with them. Stonewall Jackson was already

dead, shot by his own men in the dark, at Chancellorsville.

The silent, humorless, lemon-sucking Jackson is never portrayed as a reflective man. "Praying and fighting," wrote General Richard Taylor, "appeared to be his idea of the whole duty of man." (Too much of the South, according to its detractors, is still of the same persuasion.)

Yet it's Jackson, who never saw the end or the issue of his war, whom I'd resurrect just long enough to ask, "Was it worth it?" At Mary Baldwin the sacred flower of Southern womanhood now comes in blossoms of every color, including many descendants of the slaves whose emancipation the fallen hero opposed. At least two Mary Baldwin students have pierced their tongues, according to the dean. Well-bred Southern ladies wear the uniforms of VMI cadets. The rich Valley farmland that Jackson disputed, yard by bloody yard, is now mostly in the hands of pacifist Mennonites, farmers whose religion forbids them to bear arms in any conflict.

A century after the Secession, Robert Penn Warren called the Confederate defeat "The Great Alibi" by which the South has absolved itself of all its failures. But in spite of its resistance to change and good advice, neither the Valley nor any remaining section of the South has been spared the cultural and spiritual blight, the grim consequence of the mass-market society that Warren and his Fugitives blamed on Yankee capitalists.

Riding up his valley on old Sorrel, Jackson would recognize many of the buildings—preservation and restoration are great passions here—and not much else. Like his enemy Brown he was an exotic specimen, a nineteenth-century Christian gentleman who gave his life gladly, almost recklessly, for abstractions like freedom, honor, and Almighty God. I doubt that he could relate to many of us, or review our ranks with much satisfaction.

Eating Rats at Vicksburg

Race is like a big crazy cousin locked in the basement, a red-eyed giant who strangled a dog and crippled a policeman the last time he got loose. We never forget that he's down there. But it's amazing how long we can ignore him, no matter how much noise he makes moaning and banging on the pipes. Our denial's almost airtight, until one day he's out in the yard again swinging a pickax, and all we can do is blame each other and dial 911.

He's out. The Million Man March of Minister Farrakhan, the Simpson verdict, the ambitious black general who paralyzed both political parties with his popularity—where can you hide from race anymore? There's no safe place to position yourself, either. Sympathize with the Simpson jury and you're a misogynist; ridicule them and you're a racist. Criticize Farrakhan and you're a closet Klansman; praise him and you're an anti-Semite.

It's real hard to duck that last one, the anti-Semitism. On the day of the Million Man March, the *Chicago Tribune* quoted Quanell X, national youth minister for Farrakhan's Nation of Islam: "I say to Jewish America: Get ready . . . knuckle up, put your boots on, because we're ready and the war is going down."

"All you Jews can go straight to hell," suggested another Farrakhan aide, the virulent Khallid Muhammad.

Yet black columnists I respect compared the March to Woodstock and "the embrace of home."

"African-American men who missed it missed more than they will ever know," wrote Leonard Pitts, Jr., of the *Miami Herald*.

Where's the middle ground for the moderate and well-meaning? Race is intellectual quicksand. All the wisdom I've ever heard on the subject was personal, provisional, subject to revision. And that ambiguity runs a little thicker here in the South.

While 400,000 black men converged on Washington, several thousand of the South's best readers converged on Nashville for the Southern Festival of Books. Black readers were much in evidence. But so was the fact that even literature is segregated, unintentionally. I'm afraid I never saw a black person in line to get a book signed by a white author, or a white person in line to meet a black author. The only writer who seemed to straddle the color barrier comfortably was the inimitable Reverend Will Campbell, the last of a breed of unsentimental liberals the South will sorely miss when they're gone.

Few white writers consciously target white readers. But a white novelist from Virginia, addressing a panel on Southern literature, exposed one good reason why whites are the only readers most of them find.

She confessed her lifelong indifference to the Civil War, and her wish that we might finally bury the Confederate dead. A large all-white audience was divided between applause and horror at this revelation. But among the mildly horrified was another novelist on the panel, one of her close personal friends.

It turned out that several of the poets and novelists at the Nashville gathering can discuss Shiloh or Chickamauga regiment by regiment, hour by hour, the way my friends and I discuss a classic World Series. Some readers are afflicted even more severely. An old man came up to the writer who was tired of The War and reproached her sorrowfully, with tears in his eyes: "My family lived on rats during the siege of Vicksburg," he said, "and we've never gotten over it."

What can you say to that? I've lived in the South half my life. In none of the places where I lived the other half—not even in England, land of defiant anachronism—did I encounter anything approaching this old man's retro-fixation. Every year at the Festival of Books, historians and intellectuals gather to flog the official cult of

Southern nostalgia, as articulated by the much-deconstructed Fugitives in *I'll Take My Stand* (1930). Yet most Southern literature has been rooted in such a profound, clinging, pervasive nostalgia that's it's hard for us to imagine what could have been written without it.

"The South has been notorious for mythologizing itself," writes poet James Applewhite of North Carolina. "That part of the mind of the South which does not know itself persistently wishes to see the Old South, before the war, as a kind of Eden."

Why Dixie? Nostalgia is a function not only of culture, but of aging. It's a softening of perception few adults avoid. Just at the age when your hopes begin to lose variety and velocity, nostalgia comes to you as a friend, retouching your memories in brighter colors and air-brushing out most of the grief and humiliation.

Nostalgia is a mercy much like whiskey; it becomes a handicap when it intoxicates you and a curse when you can't sober up. You've uncorked the bottle too many times when you begin to pine for some imaginary Eden. A perfect un-Southern illustration was the political development of Irving Kristol, one of the godfathers of the "neo-conservative" movement. In a devastating review of Kristol's book, *Neoconservatism: The Autobiography of an Idea,* Theodore Draper demonstrates that Kristol's philosophy hangs entirely upon his belief in a retro never-never land—a utopia where capitalism is the genial guarantor of a humane bourgeois patriarchy, one that values and protects Jews and other industrious, orderly minorities.

In your dreams, Irving—the only place a Jew can court right-wing Christians without surrendering the last tatters of his self-respect. But Kristol's high-wire act—a blend of elaborate rationalization, selective perception, and daredevil denial—resembles tricks that intelligent Southerners have been performing all their lives.

Everyone's entitled to the symbols of his history. I have no problem with the Confederate battle flag, if you convince me that it's displayed in a nonconfrontational context. (I have no personal stake in The War; of my eight great-grandparents, only one, a woman, was living in the United States before 1870.)

But it would be a different matter, a different flag, if I were black. Novelist Jill McCorkle, a white North Carolinian, tells a story about a woman who was fawning over the Civil War historian Shelby Foote at a writer's conference.

"Oh, don't you just wish you'd been alive back in those days?" she gushed directly at a black writer, Tina McElroy Ansa, who answered simply, "No."

Literary Southerners are entitled to Stonewall Jackson and the Lost Cause. Blacks are equally entitled to view the Civil War as blessed deliverance from a society where they were bought, sold, and bred like hunting dogs, and usually treated with less affection. Most black readers don't care if *Huckleberry Finn* is great or even great-spirited literature. It embarrasses them. They don't want to "valorize" Nigger Jim. They want to forget him.

Most Southern writers I know regard themselves as racial liberals. But memory is the primary raw material of their trade. It's hard for them to see that the least blush of nostalgic longing, in a white Southerner's story, will strike many black Americans as an outright insult.

You don't have to go back 130 years, to the war and the great-grandfathers, to find the raw places. It wasn't much more than thirty years ago that my liberal hometown of Chapel Hill, so despised by Jesse Helms, was still making its bows to Jim Crow. A black man couldn't get a degree there, or a sandwich.

When Hodding Carter, Jr., entered Bowdoin College in Maine in 1923, he was such a racist that he'd get up and leave the room when the school's lone black undergraduate entered, and he avoided the toilet he thought the man was using. Carter, who became an editorial crusader for racial justice, was nine years old when he saw his first lynching victim, a black woman, hanging from a bridge near his home in Hammond, Louisiana.

Hodding Carter is not ancient history; I ate supper with his widow in New Orleans just last month. W. J. Cash, in *The Mind of the South* (1941), recalls a conversation with a night rider who had fond memories of burning a black man alive. John Egerton, in *Speak Now*

Against the Day (1994), reports that it was such a public burning in Tennessee that forged the radical conscience of H. L. Mitchell, who organized the first biracial union of Southern sharecroppers.

The last racial murder officially recorded as a lynching occurred in 1951. In nursing homes somewhere in the South, a few of the dreadful old crocodiles who carried the nooses or lit the torches must still be breathing. It's no wonder that African Americans aren't a nostalgic people. Black writers like Toni Morrison and Randall Kenan may work wonders with memory, but never accuse them of nostalgia.

Current reality isn't especially pretty, for most black Americans. One black male in three will be incarcerated at some point in his life. But Colin Powell led the presidential preference polls for six months, and only seventeen bewildered Klansmen showed up for "a mass rally" in Raleigh. Michael Jordan and Oprah Winfrey control financial empires. Clarence Thomas sits on the Supreme Court, even if he had to submit to a surgical procedure to get the nomination. O. J. Simpson can not only sleep with a white woman, but beat her up and probably even murder her without fear of being hanged from a bridge.

Don't wax too nostalgic in front of black people. They'll take the present, any day, over their American past. They don't read *Gone With the Wind* or Walker Percy, and I've got my doubts about Faulkner. I'll bet they didn't watch *The Civil War* on PBS. Don't lecture them about the Siege of Vicksburg. They think those starving Confederates deserved to eat a few rats, or worse.

The Family of Man

Students at the University of North Carolina have discovered that one of the older buildings on the hallowed Chapel Hill campus was named after a certain Colonel William Saunders, who seems to have held high office (Wizard, Dragon, Titan, Hydra, Grand Cyclops?) in the Ku Klux Klan. There's a protest movement that aims to rename Colonel Saunders's memorial after someone more sympathetic.

My view is that the current generation of undergraduates, so often indicted by their teachers and even their parents for apathy and avarice, should be encouraged in nearly any form of activism or idealism they embrace. Their hearts are in the right place, even if their discovery that racists helped to build their university is like kids in Lapland discovering snow. In this case rediscovering the obvious is better than forgetting it.

But dishonoring old Night Hawk Saunders would set a painful precedent. North Carolina would proceed from nameless buildings to a hopeless confusion of nameless streets, towns, and counties. Purging the names of unacceptable white people of previous generations is like taking an eraser to the map of the South. Georgia, Louisiana, Virginia, Maryland, and the Carolinas were all named for kings and queens. A campaign to rid us of the memory of these odious despots and parasites in their powdered wigs—these fat ghosts sneering at our freedoms—would leave the map more or less bare between Pennsylvania and the Florida line.

Personally I'd rather see buildings stripped of the names of tobacco barons, hog bosses, and union-busting mill moguls of more recent vintage and more verifiable infamy. But that's economic suicide for North Carolina colleges. Multiculturalists' protests are invariably symbolic, as symbolic and often as simplistic as their abuse of history and literature. Can't we teach students the mistakes of the past without inciting them to waste their precious indignation on the defenseless dead?

It's easier and more appropriate to judge ideas than individuals. This is no apology for the posthumously notorious Colonel Saunders. But the Ku Klux Klan is just too easy. It has no respectable defenders, it owns no controversy. It was a kind of gruesome winged insect, with a venomous sting, that grew from the worm of racism at the heart of the American experiment.

These days it's a safe target, too. The last time the Klan marched in Chapel Hill, I saw a pitiful single file of ten or eleven social rejects, just this side of ragged, with ruined teeth and malnourished children. Spectators offered to buy them some lunch, or some milk for their kids. The Klan was similarly represented at its most recent marches, in several Northern cities.

Do you know what it means, exactly, if someone tells you that your granddaddy was in the Klan? Actually there were two Klans— the one founded in Tennessee in 1865 and the revival Klan that convened at Stone Mountain, Georgia, in 1915, inspired by World War I xenophobia and D. W. Griffith's Klan-friendly *Birth of a Nation.* The first Klan was almost exclusively Southern, strongest in the Piedmont and mountain states. The second was a national movement, especially powerful in such Deep South strongholds as Indiana, Oregon, and Maine.

The Klan's secret organization was elaborate and imaginative, but no central authority prevailed. Degrees of violence and criminal activity varied widely, according to the temperaments of local initiates. For years the Klan of the second incarnation was camouflaged as a run-of-the-mill fraternal lodge. President Warren G. Harding took the Klan oath as a campaign photo opportunity, as casually as he might have donned an Indian headdress in South Dakota. In his acerbic essay "Star-Spangled Men" (1920), H. L. Mencken includes the KKK in a long list of fraternal orders he finds ridiculous, like the Odd Fellows and the Woodmen of the World.

Exposed as a former Klansman when FDR nominated him for the Supreme Court, Hugo Black asked the country to believe that he was never a night rider, just another ambitious young Alabama politician sniffing the wind. He was forgiven and confirmed. At the time of Black's membership, in the early '20s, the second Klan claimed five million members, an Invisible Empire indeed when the population of the USA was 100 million.

So you don't really know, unless he left a diary, whether the Klansman in your family tree was a church-burning murderer or some timid small-town pharmacist trying to preserve his trade.

You know he was wrong. But it's easy to go wrong in a crowd. A friend of mine, a Jew, says he measures an individual by one moral yardstick—whether that person would have hidden him from the Gestapo. A tough call, in any case. But naturally all of us who hear this are confident that we have passed his test. Too confident, probably. The other night I heard a group of men—middle-aged professors, liberals—agree that they, as Germans, would probably have gone along with the Nazi program.

Impressed by their candor, I was distressed by the implications. Would my Jewish friend have been surprised at all? Few of us can imagine ourselves goose-stepping, Heil-Hitlering, or kicking in doors in the ghetto. But speaking out, resisting, once the consequences of doing so were clearly established? That takes a hero—in Berlin in 1938, in Selma, Alabama, in 1920—or in 1965.

Heroes are rare; hypocrites, pharisees, and safe-distance moralizers breed like fleas in cheap apartments. Students are ill-served by ideologues who squeeze history into classic plot lines, all martyrs and monsters. History is no morality play. Relativity rears its ugly head, and ambiguity chews its weary way through the most resplendent ideology. For an extreme example, take slavery, the most satanic institution that ever squandered the moral capital of a "Christian"

society. The United States may never recover from it. But slavery was-
n't a white man's institution; England came to it late, when it became
obvious that indentured servants and the scrapings of prisons and
poorhouses would never meet the demand for labor in her American colonies. Europeans, with their avarice and organization, were
the trunk and branches of the slave trade. Its roots, as every historian knows, were the tribal wars and raids that bled West Africa for
centuries.

Only a handful of Europeans took the high risks upriver, in the
jungles Joseph Conrad mythologizes in *The Heart of Darkness*. Black
people sold black people into slavery. And as Rwanda's Hutus and
Tutsis still demonstrate, slavery wasn't the worst thing that happened
to the losers in Africa's wars.

No work of literature offers more devastating images of the slave
trade than Barry Unsworth's *Sacred Hunger* (1992). Its English pro-
tagonist, Dr. Paris, is sickened to the verge of suicide by what he sees
on his uncle's slave ship, and by his own guilt as a party to it. But he
can't ignore the callousness with which Africans doom each other, or
the tribal animosities that survive even the shared agony of the slave
ships.

"Because they all have black faces we suppose them close in fellowship," Paris writes in his journal. "But when have we been so towards people only because they are white-skinned like ourselves. I
have not noticed much affection and loyalty among us towards the
Dutch or the French."

A Caucasian weary of "white devil" rhetoric will point out that it
was white people, in both England and the United States, who even-
tually outlawed slavery. (Wasn't there a war?) To the best of my knowledge, there was never a Pan-African movement to cut off the slave
trade at its roots.

The unscrupulous prey on the weak, then and now, and sometimes the roles are reversed. The unwelcome truth is that victimhood
confers no moral advantage. African complicity in no way alleviates
the guilt of white slavers. But it casts doubt on conventional wisdom

about racist psychology, the received truth that human beings need to "dehumanize" other races in order to exploit and destroy them.

What does this mean, to dehumanize? In New Guinea, Australian zoologist Tim Flannery *(Throwim Way Leg,* 1998) discovered a tribe that until the 1960s regularly raided neighboring villages to slaughter, gut, and dismember all the adult inhabitants. Then they carried home the meat to feed them through the rainy season.

This might seem to be the last word in dehumanizing an enemy, when he becomes your dinner. Yet the children of the victims were adopted by the cannibals and raised as their own. Flannery meets one such orphan, nurtured with the greatest devotion by the couple who ate his parents. ("They were fat," recalls his stepmom. "They gave me all the milk I needed to nourish two children.")

To foreign eyes, these tribes are identical. It puts race in a different perspective.

Racism, xenophobia, is universal among the tribes of man. It's a stubborn, discouraging reality. But because it rests on an abstraction—perceived differences, perceived kinship—perhaps it's not one of the biggest realities. Not compared with callous self-interest or simple, practical *need,* which explains both slavers and cannibals. Maybe it's optimistic to believe that we need to see our victims as subhuman inferiors. If there's any fixed truth about the dark and unpredictable human heart, it may be more frightening by far.

The Unteachables

A few miles south of the state zoo at Asheboro, a well-paved country road winds into the Uwharrie Mountains. At the edge of Uwharrie National Forest, a nondescript highway bridge crosses a narrow branch of the Little River. But a gravel road on the left takes you to its photogenic predecessor, one of two surviving covered bridges in North Carolina.

The bridge is endangered. Time and the weather are implacable enemies of a wooden bridge that was built when William Howard Taft was president. But the Pisgah Covered Bridge has had friends to look out for it. In 1970 it was listed on the National Registry of Historic Places, and the North Carolina Department of Transportation recently spent $18,000 to restore it—a generous investment in a bridge that cost $40 to build in 1910.

The main timbers look indestructible. Natural decrepitude is not the problem. The problem is that the new tin roof is generously ventilated with bullet holes, planks have been scavenged for campfires and the walls are covered with a disfiguring rash of inane and obscene graffiti, like a Manhattan subway tunnel ("Lisa loves Dude," "Michele loves Jose," "Wetbacks suck," "Rasta Babes Rule"). Sunlight pierces the cool, dark tunnel through hundreds of perforations; I lack the forensic skills to distinguish bullet holes from knotholes.

People have worked hard to preserve the Pisgah Covered Bridge. Other people are working hard to reduce it to a pile of splinters. It's a striking illustration of Southern contrariness, a lesson for visitors who would like to get beyond our stereotypes.

No one reveres the past more than Southerners. Go to Charleston, Savannah, Richmond, colonial Williamsburg, even little Natchez, Mississippi, and observe the immaculate shrines of our ancestor worship. New Englanders are Bedouin nomads by comparison.

No one honors history more faithfully than one kind of Southerner; no one erases it more quickly than another kind. For every authentic Southerner who spends Sundays pulling weeds in the Confederate cemetery, there's one equally authentic who likes to shoot the crosses off the headstones. If you're obsessed with race, like most Hollywood movies about the South, you miss the nuances of the caste system. This is all between white people.

The silliest stereotypes contain subatomic particles of the truth. In the New South you won't find any characters familiar from *Gone With the Wind,* or familiar from *God's Little Acre,* either. But you may see where Margaret Mitchell and Erskine Caldwell got their ideas.

Notice the rich variety of insulting names for poor whites: Rednecks and lintheads (farmers and textile workers), peckerwoods, hillbillies, crackers, woolhats, po' white trash, and several I forget. Wops, Micks, kikes, and Polacks were Northern coinage. Southerners saved their meanest slang for members of their own ethnic group.

The South had class problems from the start, when one set of ancestors arrived with royal land grants and another arrived as exiled convicts and indentured servants. One set owned land, mills, and slaves; the other struggled to feed their children. The gap between blue collar and starched collar stretched wider here than in any other part of the colonies, and like nearly everything historical, the South has managed to preserve it. To compare the descendants of Ashley Wilkes and Ty Ty Walden, visit the Masters in Augusta and then the Diehard 500 at Talladega.

The great plantations are gone, but descendants of the cotton aristocracy—lawyers, bankers, manufacturers—still own the best land and the biggest houses. They send their children away to school and still manage, in many places, to run things much as their ancestors did when they owned villages and whole counties outright.

At the nether end of the system, where Hindus place the untouchables, Dixie maintains its own hereditary underclass. I call them the unteachables—whites who won't grasp the critical fact that it isn't black people who are keeping them down. These are the rednecks Jeff Foxworthy celebrates, but I doubt that many of them buy his books. If they hold history in contempt or utter disregard, it's because they didn't own any of it. They were sharecroppers. To them, the good old days was that Golden Age before Northern liberals cancelled *Hee Haw* and *The Dukes of Hazzard.*

From the beginning, these two sets of distant cousins had nothing in common except their color. The Civil War was the last time they really cooperated, and that took something of a con job. The few Southerners who faced real economic hardship from emancipation convinced the rest that Lincoln was coming down to sign over what little they had—dirty jobs, hardscrabble farms—to emancipated slaves. It worked then, and racialist demagogues kept it working for another 130 years.

Some say Jesse Helms is working it still. Few unteachables ever make the logical, radical connection that could trump the race card. The economic common cause, uniting poor whites and blacks and now Hispanics, is more of a pipe dream now than it was in the '30s.

But the redneck must sense that he's been snookered. Preservationists suppose that people who shoot covered bridges are just no-account and disrespectful. There may be more to it than that. What peasantry, even under feudalism, waited longer for its chance than the South's poor whites? And to them the New South looks like another wave of carpetbaggers, golfers from everywhere and nowhere waiting to take over when the landed gentry finally peters out.

Cheated of their birthright, frustrated in every populist uprising— Huey Long and George Wallace were shot, the same as Martin Luther King, Jr., and Medgar Evers—unteachables rebel in small ways. No covered bridge, no granite monument or lovingly restored plantation house is safe from their shotguns and their magic markers.

The Twelve Apostles

Not long ago, my wife and I moved into a house in Hillsborough, North Carolina, that was built before the Civil War. It's of no special interest to historians, as far as we know. But it has an aura. It belonged to a family of undertakers, for one thing. My bedroom overlooks an eighteenth-century cemetery, where a signer of the Declaration of Independence is interred along with Confederate officers, antebellum governors, and the like. We own a decrepit red carriage house from a previous century and an ancient freestone wall half-buried under honeysuckle, and out back a brick summer kitchen, older than the house, where someone's slaves cooked supper when Andrew Jackson was president.

Crooked trees, stripped and maimed by the hurricane, give the place an Addams Family atmosphere. A friend, only half joking, tells me I've come to rest where I belong—in a decommissioned mortuary with a view of the graveyard.

History has tightened its grip on me. Don't look for me on horseback next spring, dressed for a Civil War reenactment. But those accountants brandishing bayonets don't seem quite as silly as they used to.

History lives in the bricks and stones. For a price, established by a realtor, you can listen to those stones day and night. In the South, as so many writers have noted, they never shut up. Many Southerners pay a price for listening. I can't forget the old man who said his family never recovered from eating rats at Vicksburg, or my readers' fury when I reported his anguish ironically.

"The general impression outside the South is that the South has never stopped looking back," Walker Percy wrote in 1957. "The truth, at least in my experience, is that the Southerner never thinks about the Civil War—until he finds himself among Northerners."

This may be true, but it's also true that exasperating encounters with Yankees have multiplied since 1957. Just last month in New York, two friends of mine—one from Georgia and the other from Minnesota—measured each other across the dinner table in a bistro on Madison Avenue.

"You're damn right I eat grits," the Bulldog barked at the Gopher. "Would you ask an Italian if he really ate pasta?"

Bloodshed was averted, but the spirit of 1863 had risen up in an instant, between neighbors sharing a bottle of Sauvignon Blanc. The Midwesterner had meant no harm; maybe his tone was a little condescending. If the Southerner carries a chip on his shoulder, he saves it for mixed company like this. And the past—hell, The War—is still attached to his resentment.

This astonishes Yankees. In the North, East, and West, amnesia is epidemic. William Westmoreland has been forgotten, never mind Nathan Bedford Forrest. It's only in the South that the past is a cause, an industry, an institution, a constant companion who's not always soft-spoken and discreet. The easy explanation—"Because we lost"— is also put forward to account for the disproportionate number of writers and poets the Confederate states keep producing.

My theory gives more weight to the Fugitives. Vanderbilt's rebel poets published their Agrarian manifesto, *I'll Take My Stand,* in 1930. Its immediate impact was negligible and much of its sentiment sounds antediluvian to modern ears. But a detective assigned to determine why the South is the South will find Fugitive fingerprints everywhere.

Even death hasn't silenced them. Donald Davidson's *The Big Ballad Jamboree,* a country music novel discovered among his papers at Vanderbilt, was published in 1996 by the University Press of Mississippi. My wife reviewed it for *The Journal of Country Music* and found it "too overtly thematic for my taste"—a verdict that surprised no one who remembered Donald Davidson.

This was "the unreconstructed Southerner," as Percy labeled him, who alone among the poets never backed away from *I'll Take My Stand,* not even from the language that sugarcoated Jim Crow. Davidson's return to the literary lists may spur another generation to read the book—published exactly midway in time between Appomattox and the present—that drew the permanent battle lines between the North and the South.

If you took this book today and tossed it into the faculty lounge, even in a Deep South university, it would be like throwing a slaughtered lamb into a cage of starving panthers. The walls would be coated with blood and fur and saliva. Racist, sexist, elitist, paternalist, colonialist—it's all of those, and even "fascist" has often been piled on, especially by those who misread John Gould Fletcher: "The inferior, whether in life or education, should exist only for the sake of the superior." (Fletcher's talking about a hierarchy of human qualities, not of human beings. But if you study the complete poetic works of Donald Davidson, which deify the Aryan "Tall Men" who settled Tennessee, you're bound to be reminded of another group of theorizing Aryans who were raising more hell than white Southerners in the year 1930.)

If you're a Southerner, reading *I'll Take My Stand* is facing up to your grandfather, warts and all. Conceived as a *cri de coeur* against the industrialization and urbanization that had begun to disfigure the Old South, these twelve essays include some of the most shameless aristocratic hogwash you'll ever encounter in print. William F. Buckley himself might shy from the following, by Stark Young of Mississippi: "He [the Anglo-Saxon] is saved, if at all, only by a ruling better class, whose stately or unholy views keep the masses somewhat in awe."

Whoa, hoss. Talleyrand couldn't say it better. In our age, even monarchists seem to pay lip service to mob democracy. But *I'll Take*

My Stand mainly stinks of youth—arrogance, vanity, half-baked ideology, florid overstatement, and an impossible high-mindedness we usually call preciousness today.

They spoke for almost no one but themselves. They weren't farmers, their critics objected, but intellectuals from the rural gentry. It was the intellectual humiliation of the South during the Scopes "monkey trial," in 1925, that had provoked the Fugitives and their friends. Their manifesto neglected the real crisis of the hour, the Great Depression triggered by the stock market crash the previous fall. Other young writers of great ability—including T. S. Eliot and Lewis Mumford—were dealing more compellingly with the specter of a soiled, soulless, anonymous post-industrial society.

The Fugitives were young and isolated, and their timing was poor. The greatest writer among them, the twenty-five-year-old Robert Penn Warren, later repudiated much of his essay on race. Allen Tate came to describe Agrarianism as a metaphor, not an ideology. John Crowe Ransom, who wrote the keynote essay, distanced himself from the Agrarian program after he left Vanderbilt for Kenyon.

How has this obscure little book, half disowned by its authors, come to rank second only to W. J. Cash's *The Mind of the South* in defining Southerners?

For one thing, they lived very long lives, the Fugitives and their friends and disciples. I had the pleasure of meeting Warren when he was in his eighties, and it wasn't two years ago that I poured a glass of bourbon for the last of the original essayists, the late Andrew Lytle. As writers, teachers, and editors they dominated the journals, the best universities, and the Southern literary canon for decades, spreading their peculiar gospel of ancestor worship and pugnacious resistance to Yankee notions of progress. In the South there's scarcely a high-school English teacher, of a certain age, whose academic pedigree doesn't hook up somewhere with one of the Twelve Apostles.

Southerners have a weakness for religion. And in no other region, in no other intellectual establishment was there ever a secular faith that went beyond ancestor worship and offered its own reactionary theology—the past (agrarian, antebellum) as heaven and the future (urban, industrial) as hell.

Paradise Lost, period. You didn't have to be too clever to figure out who played the devil. Agrarian theology sanctified nostalgia and influenced generations of Southerners who would never have endorsed it directly. Nearly all segregationists have defined themselves as traditionalists, not racists.

But it wouldn't be haunting us still, this strange faith of our fathers, if it hadn't turned out to be so prophetic. The worst the Apostles predicted has come to pass.

"Industrialism is rightfully a menial, of almost miraculous cunning but no intelligence," warned John Crowe Ransom. "It needs to be strongly governed or it will destroy the economy of the household." Industrial society amounted to "an unrelenting war on nature," in Ransom's view. Even advertising was reviled as the voice of Satan, by these men who had never seen TV. It's strange that anticorporate, anti-materialistic, pro-environment opinions are never described as conservative anymore.

All the Fugitives lived to see the Fall of the South, and the rest of the country, to the devils they had named. The center has not held, not even in their heartland. Most of the South now belongs to the party of Lincoln, which takes its marching orders straight from Wall Street. In this morning's paper, I saw where the mayor of Raleigh is trying to blackmail businessmen into buying $50,000 luxury boxes to support major-league hockey in our capital.

Hockey?

And my daughter tells me that she can log onto the Internet in her office at the University of North Carolina and call up graphic depictions of every sexual perversion dark hearts have devised.

There are some things, thank God, Donald Davidson didn't live to see. Sitting in my old house next to the cemetery, I'm slowly, sadly, coming to appreciate his point of view.

From Auschwitz to Alabama

It was scarcely a pause in the dizzy circus of sex scandals. But President Clinton's official apology to the survivors of the infamous Tuskegee syphilis study offered a rare, almost nostalgic glimpse of human dignity in a public arena monopolized by exhibitionists and voyeurs.

"It is never too late to work to restore faith and trust," said Herman Shaw, ninety-five, accepting the president's apology on behalf of eight survivors and 391 other black Alabamans, now deceased, who were human guinea pigs in a Nazi-style experiment conducted by the U.S. Public Health Service. "In order for America to reach its full potential," Shaw concluded, "we must truly be one America, black, red, white together . . . never allowing the kind of tragedy which happened to us to happen again."

The words and sentiments are familiar. We've been hearing them all our lives. But never, until now, from ordinary working men (not criminals or mental patients like previous victims of America's Dr. Mengeles) who were recruited by their own government to die untreated of a disease that's been entirely curable since 1947. They qualified by virtue of their race and their poverty.

"What the United States did was shameful, and I am sorry," President Clinton told Shaw and four other ancient survivors, gathered in the East Room of the White House. "The U.S. government did something that was wrong—deeply, profoundly, morally wrong."

Apologies cost nothing, the cynic reminds us. No one will go to prison for this appalling official crime that was terminated, after forty years, in 1972. But the United States has put some money where its mouth is—at least $10 million so far to settle a class action suit filed by the victims and their heirs.

Apologies are always too little and too late; scoundrels toss them around like party favors. But I've noticed that a little contrition, sincerely expressed, can be contagious. Two days after the president's apology to Herman Shaw, four South Carolina bishops, representing the Catholic, Lutheran, Anglican, and Methodist churches, issued a joint apology for their "sin of racism."

A week later, British Prime Minister Tony Blair apologized to the Irish for the Great Potato Famine of the 1840s. Contrition is in the air and it's possible, though unlikely, that the South Carolina bishops will shame some Christian politicians into the confessional. Actually there's only one powerful member of the old Jim Crow Gang who has never apologized, to the best of my knowledge. George Wallace said he was sorry. Even Strom Thurmond disowned his racist ways as the reckless folly of his long-ago youth.

Only Jesse Helms, chairman of the Foreign Relations Committee, seems likely to die with his sins unconfessed. We have a dream, here in North Carolina. History's most vivid image of contrition is the Holy Roman Emperor Henry IV kneeling in the snow at Canossa, begging the forgiveness of Pope Gregory. In our dream Jesse Helms is kneeling in the snow at Grandfather Mountain—but even a shag rug in Raleigh would be fine—receiving absolution from Jesse Jackson.

We have a dream.

Apology eases the conscience, lifts the spirit, clears the air. Sometimes it opens floodgates of memory and remorse. And racism is America's original sin, a bitter quarrel with Almighty God that began long before the first slave ship sailed into Charleston harbor. It commenced with the first Native American a white man cheated, raped, or murdered.

The purest essence of racial insanity is the white Christian who sincerely believes he's going to heaven, and just as sincerely believes he'll find it segregated. But white Southerners, particularly those whose adulthood began after 1968, have grown very weary of apologizing for segregation.

We're innocent, most of us, of overt racism or of supporting overt racists—though most of us have friends who belong to all-white country clubs. In our innocence, we're easily wounded by stereotypes. But just as white policemen and cab drivers have such a hard time distinguishing black college students from black thugs, African Americans have a hard time distinguishing white liberals from our fathers and grandfathers.

Military bases, like North Carolina's Fort Bragg, still harbor white supremacists and skinheads who commit hate crimes. Black churches still burn mysteriously, though most of the hard cash for rebuilding them, nearly a million dollars, has come from the right-wing Christian Coalition.

Race draws a fine line between healthy remorse and neurotic guilt—a line Southerners walk more carefully than many Northern liberals, who evolved from the cringing apologies of the '60s to a smug self-righteousness that fights racism by heaping prizes on black artists or making stupid films about the savage South. The Tuskegee experiment is a huge submerged iceberg of guilt, and scholars will take an intense interest in the way America divides it up and passes it around.

The biggest sins aren't necessarily the hardest ones to hide. The more people with a vested interest in suppressing the sin, the deeper the hole where we'll find it buried. Like those Nazi bank accounts that keep surfacing to indict the gnomes of Zurich, Tuskegee is an evil that was buried deep because so many respectable citizens had so much to lose. It's still hard to believe that no one broke the silence for forty years—not physicians savaging their Hippocratic Oaths, not bureaucrats playing the Angel of Death in Alabama, with Auschwitz so fresh in their minds. The revelation isn't that black people's lives were traded at such a discount, compared with the lives of whites. We've read Toni Morrison. The revelation is that so many American doctors and civil servants could hold any human life so cheaply.

When did harmless people suffer a more cynical betrayal of their trust? Here's your government, which demands such loyalty that it may ask you to lay down your life to prove it. Here's your doctor, who always has your life in his hands. And to them, if you're Herman Shaw, you have no greater value than a rat in a cage.

Another element of betrayal was almost as cruel. The Tuskegee experiment was launched in the last days of the Hoover administration, but implemented in all its malevolence under Franklin D. Roosevelt. In spite of historians who note that he courted Dixiecrats and never backed an antilynching law, FDR was almost universally regarded as the black's first friend in the White House. When was the last time you met a black man with the Christian name Hoover, or Coolidge?

It's a Southern embarrassment that the experiment occurred in Alabama and at Tuskegee, site of the famous black college founded by Booker T. Washington. There's no evidence that Tuskegee Institute was involved, though it wouldn't surprise a reader of *Invisible Man,* with Ralph Ellison's devastating portrait of the Uncle Toms of Tuskegee, educators more outraged by nappy hair than cracker condescension. Ellison was an undergraduate at Tuskegee, studying music and poetry, when the PHS began its "Study of Untreated Syphilis in the Negro Male."

Could it have happened, and stayed a secret for forty years, in Detroit? That's not clear. The U.S. Public Health Service was not controlled by Alabama racists, or in collaboration with them. These sweet doctors were most attracted, it appears, by a passive, impoverished rural population with no tradition of standing up for itself.

I don't see the Tuskegee horror as an indictment of Alabama, of the South, or of our grandparents, none of whom knew the first thing about evil experiments conducted by federal agencies. If a Southerner wants to refine and educate his guilt (and mix it with some pride), he should read John Egerton's *Speak Now Against the Day* (1994), which tells another story of the 1930s. Along with his tribute to heroic Southerners who took a stand for racial equality many years before the civil rights movement, Egerton sets the record straight—who helped, who was decent but timid, who was really a part of the problem.

It wasn't a North-South thing, Tuskegee. It was an example of the worst that can happen when a toxin like racism falls into the hands of the most repulsive human subgroup this side of night riders and church-burners. We all know them. They throw you out of school for smoking a cigarette, downsize you when your wife is pregnant, give you twenty years for a few ounces of dope, stick pins in a map to indicate where boys in uniforms are bleeding to death. They sit cold and bloodless as yesterday's pork roast and decide your fate.

One phase is The Eternal Official, who terrified Kafka; another is the hard-eyed Man of Science. Every race, region and ethnic group produces them. Bureaucracies attract and promote them. They don't make the rules, they just enforce them. They don't invent the nightmare schemes, they just implement them. As one who could never send a single blameless basset hound to his fate in an animal lab—not under strictest orders from the Pope—I've always been acutely aware of the bloodless ones and the difference between them and me.

The cold ones don't always rise to the level of deciding life and death. But when they do, take cover. No matter who the doctor is, no matter whose flag he's waving, get a second opinion. Beyond black and white, that's the lesson from Tuskegee.

Requiem for a Bantamweight

The little bulldog has made his last headlines, and they were inadequate. Coinciding exactly with the loathsome climax to the most bizarre, corrosive sex scandal in American history, the death of George Wallace was almost overlooked by the overheated media machinery. Coked up on legal pornography, free at last from the burdens of memory or responsibility, the national media barely looked up from their keyholes to acknowledge the death of a sick old man in a wheelchair, a politician whose last run for office was in 1982. In the hysteria of yet another tabloid stampede, few hands were available to accord this singular life the editorial consideration it deserved. A year ago the same thing happened to Mother Teresa, an irony Governor Wallace would have appreciated.

You were cheated, George. I remember when they wouldn't leave you alone. But you died in a state of dignity, you old SOB, holding your head higher than most of your newsroom enemies, those city Yankees who treated you like the slimiest thing to crawl out of Dixie since Simon Legree.

Journalist Teddy White, who made a career of presidential politics, dismissed George Wallace as "a narrow-minded, grossly provincial man" and "a Southern populist of the meanest streak."

But where, now, is the liberal press that installed Teddy White as a guru—and where is the presidency?

Only the historians are left to judge George Wallace now. They'll rank him—serious historians have already ranked him—as one of the most influential political figures of the twentieth century. As a fledgling moderate in a state dominated by white racists, young Wallace took his first electoral licking and swore his famous oath that he'd never be "out-niggered" by another political opponent.

"I started out talking about schools and highways and prisons and taxes, and I couldn't make them listen," he once confessed ruefully to an Alabama newspaper editor. "Then I began talking about niggers—and they stomped the floor."

Wallace fashioned himself into a fire-breathing segregationist who came to own the state of Alabama as completely as Huey Long once owned Louisiana. His favorite speechwriter, author of Wallace's defiant "Segregation now . . . segregation tomorrow . . . segregation forever!" was Asa "Ace" Carter, a ferocious Klan terrorist linked to the 1956 castration of a retarded black handyman, a victim chosen at random as a warning to "troublemakers." (In one of history's more improbable footnotes, Ace Carter fled to Texas and shed his Alabama identity like a snakeskin. He became Forrest Carter, the "Native American" author of a best-selling novel, *The Education of Little Tree,* the high-minded story of a young Cherokee's coming-of-age.)

Those were ugly times in Alabama, and George Wallace made himself as ugly as his tireless ambition required. The divisive politics he perfected were nothing new in his part of the South. But Wallace preached his white supremacy with a soulful blend of heartfelt populism, a little man's fierce determination to fight the system that sold him short.

It was a blend that mobilized resentful underdogs wherever he took his message. If the pitch was tailored to suit his audience, there was nothing calculating about the pit-bull pugnacity Wallace radiated. As a pint-sized teenager he was one of the most celebrated boxers in the South, twice bantamweight Golden Gloves champion of Alabama, runner-up in the 1936 Southern finals in Nashville. An indomitable counterpuncher, Wallace was defeated just four times in his life. That belligerent thrust of his jaw, interpreted by gentler souls as pure redneck meanness, said to Americans with hard lives and losing records that he was a champion who could take a punch and never quit on them.

Wallace came as close as any overtly racist politician to convert-ing America to the wisdom of Old Alabama. As a third-party candi-date for president, he was primarily responsible for the Waterloo of American liberalism, the narrow defeat of Hubert Humphrey in 1968. In 1972, Wallace dominated the Democratic primaries until he was shot in Maryland in May. According to historian Dan T. Carter (in his Wallace biography, *The Politics of Rage),* these Wallace campaigns in-spired Richard Nixon—at the urging of speechwriter Pat Buchanan—to adopt his successful "Southern strategy" of 1972.

In direct consequence, Carter argues, reactionaries seized the Re-publican Party, American electoral politics underwent permanent re-alignment, and an unlikely alliance between Wall Street and Tobacco Road elected Ronald Reagan. ("Wall Street," wrote Lillian Smith, "—that fabulous crooked canyon of evil winding endlessly through the Southern mind.")

This unnatural alliance is the most dominant force—some would say the most toxic force—in national politics today. Dan Carter says we owe it all to George Wallace. A yellow-dog Democrat who grew up worshipping Franklin Delano Roosevelt, Wallace was the model and catalyst for a right-wing revolution that swept away nearly everything the New Deal espoused or achieved. But in farewell we should note that the governor was always true, in his fashion, to his beloved FDR. He was ever the populist who took his guidance from the man in the street.

It was the Republican Party and its surviving racialist demagogues, like Jesse Helms, who devised the post-populist Raw Deal—a cor-porate fast shuffle that promises poor whites nothing whatsoever ex-cept a worse deal for black people. And still it works, as George Wal-lace could have predicted from his first political lesson in Alabama long ago. Pat Buchanan, ironically, is the only Republican who still whistles a populist tune.

Wallace watched most of this from a wheelchair. Crippled by an as-sassin's bullets at the height of his influence—he'd just won a primary in Michigan and finished second in Pennsylvania and Indiana—he recovered enough to make a die-hard last run at the presidency in

1976. He never relinquished his grip on Alabama, not until age and chronic pain took the edge off his lifelong hunger to rule the roost.

In his suffering, dreadful by all accounts, Wallace converted to a new vision of racial harmony. He disavowed the politics of rage and made public acts of contrition to black leaders like Jesse Jackson. There were those who remained skeptical about the sincerity of Wallace's conversion. Dan Carter quotes a Wallace aide, John Kohn, who said, "Hell, George could believe whatever he needed to believe." But the black voters of Alabama believed him, enough to give him 90 percent of their votes the last time he was elected governor, in 1982.

He had a hell of a life when you think about it, a life with drama, sweep, tragedy, agony, redemption. It was a big life, a big role for a little man, a farmer's son (but a doctor's grandson) from Clio, Alabama. The cast of characters was fascinating, with friends and enemies of equal luster. John F. Kennedy detested Wallace and refused to be photographed with him; a hidden photographer with a telephoto lens captured their one recorded handshake, as JFK disembarked from an Army helicopter on his Alabama visit of May 1963. Elvis Presley loved George Wallace and often sought his advice. Elvis once swore he'd personally kill Arthur Bremer, the gunman who paralyzed Wallace in 1972.

The bantamweight from Clio has thrown his last punch. Under normal circumstances this would be an occasion for stock-taking, a time when the South might find some satisfaction in a moral inventory. The most vivid symbol of its ancestral transgressions is gone— and he departed repentant, shriven and forgiven and ready for whatever grace the next place allows.

In states where juries routinely acquitted unrepentant Klan killers, a new generation of jurors and prosecutors has snatched some of the old dragons from their cozy retirement and sent them where they belong. In 1994 a Mississippi jury convicted Medgar Evers's murderer, Byron De La Beckwith. In Hattiesburg, Mississippi, a jury of six blacks, five whites and an Asian found onetime Imperial Wizard Samuel Bowers, seventy-three, guilty of the firebombing murder of

Vernon Dahmer, Sr., in 1966. In South Carolina, a jury assessed punitive damages of $38 million against Klansmen who burned a black church in 1995.

The voice—the voice of the killer Klansman that Eudora Welty reproduced so chillingly in her story "Where Is the Voice Coming From?"—that voice isn't much more than a whisper now. The South still leads the nation in murder, by a wide margin, but the murder rate has fallen 25 percent since 1978, and in most cases blacks and whites murder their own. A black historian from my own Carolina neighborhood, John Hope Franklin, chaired the President's elite panel on racial relations in America. Politically correct critics who deny that we've seen any racial progress are as irritating as the fools who say everything is fine.

Journalist John Egerton said recently in Chapel Hill that it would be "a wonderful irony" if Southerners were the ones to lead the rest of the nation toward a resolution of our economic and racial inequalities. Isn't it pretty to think so? But I see a more somber irony. By the time the Old Confederacy has made full amends for its sins—all the amends it can make at this point, or could be expected to make—the Republic it rejoined in 1865 will be so far gone to other false gods and fierce creeds, there'll be no one around to accept our credentials and declare us healed. I don't know how you feel about Washington, about the people who make the news there, or the people who report it. But if those are the people who set the moral bar Southerners are supposed to vault over, it might be high time to consider a second Act of Secession. It's a response George Wallace, always Washington's nemesis and nightmare, would understand as well as Jefferson Davis.

The Last Southern Hero

Maybe it's a deliberate provocation to style Frank M. Johnson, Jr., "the last Southern hero." It invites conflict with people who hold to different definitions of "hero," others who hold to rigid definitions of "Southern." But I have a strong case to argue, and Judge Johnson, on his part, never shrank from conflict when the case before him was a strong one.

Martin Luther King called him "a man who gave true meaning to the word 'justice.'" Among Southern liberals and veterans of the civil rights movement, Johnson has been a gigantic figure since the '50s, when his landmark rulings as a federal judge for the Middle District of Alabama established him as Jim Crow's most powerful natural enemy.

"The most influential, innovative, controversial trial judge in the United States," Alabama Senator Howell Heflin called Johnson. *Time* magazine, in a 1967 cover story, hailed him as "one of the most important men in America." To Robert F. Kennedy, Jr., one of Johnson's biographers, "he's as much an American hero as the leaders of the Revolutionary War and the Civil War."

"If he had been born one hundred years earlier he would have been Abraham Lincoln, or vice versa," Bill Moyers enthused after his interview with Johnson.

America has experienced some sea changes since the high tide of Frank Johnson's influence. Judicial activism, which he personified, is in darkest disfavor with a conservative Supreme Court. Affirmative action, which in many jurists' eyes was Johnson's personal invention, is rejected by a majority and detested as the devil's worst work by the judge's own Republican Party. The party of Lincoln to which he was devoted has become the party of Jesse Helms, David Duke, and the whole rabble of Dixiecrat racialists he labored to frustrate and defeat.

These sea changes haven't eroded Johnson's legacy, which has been written into law and legal precedent that a century of political reaction won't eradicate. But they've reduced public consciousness of his achievements, chipped away at his myth. It's as if a nation of backsliders, ashamed to look its judicial conscience square in the eye—Johnson's laser blue eyes that drove weak lawyers to wet themselves—had left his portrait hanging but turned it to the wall.

When Johnson died this summer, at eighty, America was too wrapped up in the death of John F. Kennedy, Jr., to pay much attention. Judge Johnson outlived, by nearly a year, his lifelong nemesis George Wallace, whose death in 1998 was similarly obscured by the tabloid abomination historians will be forced to call the Lewinsky Impeachment. In a thirty-year morality play with the soul of the South in the balance, Frank Johnson played the white knight and George Wallace wore black, and the issue that was decided between these onetime friends and law school classmates was arguably the most important issue America resolved in our lifetime. Their duel made compelling history and classic drama, but by the time these epic antagonists took their final curtain call, everyone had left the theater.

"Timing is everything," Johnson might have said, with laconic humility. He could use that for an epitaph. It was perfect timing—for a lone Eisenhower Republican in all-Democratic Alabama—that made him a U.S. Attorney at thirty-four and a federal judge at thirty-seven, the youngest one in the country. It was perfect timing, for the segregated and intimidated black people of Alabama, that placed Johnson on the court in 1955, just in time to teach George Wallace that the Supreme Court was serious about *Brown vs. the Board of Education*. A self-styled hillbilly from Northern Alabama, Johnson arrived in Montgomery with no debts or ties to the Democratic establishment, and when the civil rights wars came to Alabama his singularity made all the difference.

It was poor timing, on the other hand, when surgery on a near-fatal aneurysm in 1977 forced him to resign his nomination as director of the FBI. And poor timing again when Jimmy Carter's defeat in 1980, along with the right-wing takeover of the Republican Party, left him without a friend in the White House at a time when he was clearly the leading candidate for the next vacancy on the U.S. Supreme Court. It was tragic poor timing, in 1975, when Johnson arrived a minute too late to prevent his son Johnny, his only child, from locking himself in their house and committing suicide with a shotgun.

Frank Johnson was the last Southern hero because we're suffering a general extinction of heroes, along with the apparent extinction of the individual and the meaningful community (it was reported that millions mourned JFK, Jr., in Internet chat rooms—a glutinous mass of media slaves mourning a man they never met with people they've never seen). But ultimately he's our last hero because we've come to the end of the time when the South's problems are unique to the South.

Timing is everything, for heroes. In drab times, heroes-who-might-have-been file by untested, unsuspected, unfulfilled. In an age of computers, Hercules would be a terrorist or a professional wrestler. Frank Johnson was lucky, if that's the right word, to have walked onstage at a moment in history when a great judge could play a critical role.

Biographers have made much of the fact that Johnson was born and raised in rural Winston County, an enclave of hardcase North Alabama hill farmers who owned few slaves and objected so strenuously to secession that they assembled at Looney's Tavern in 1862, 2,500 strong, and declared their intention to secede from the state of Alabama. "The Free State of Winston" never saw the light of day, but most Winston men enlisted in the Union Army, more than twice as many as the Confederacy recruited. Two volunteers for the First Alabama Cavalry Regiment of the United States Army were Reuben and Moses Johnson, Frank Johnson's great-great-uncles, who came home from the war to find that rebel sympathizers had stolen all their horses and cattle (they reclaimed them at gunpoint).

Johnson's family tree is crawling with ferocious independents, lone wolves, and outright contrarians. His maternal great-grandfather, Francis Marion Treadaway, fought for the Confederacy but distinguished himself as a sheriff who routed the Ku Klux Klan; his father, Frank Johnson, Sr., was once the only Republican in the Alabama legislature. But the virtues and attitudes that set Frank Johnson apart are ones many small-town, up-country Americans can find in themselves.

Johnson's biographer Jack Bass *(Taming the Storm: The Life and Times of Judge Frank M. Johnson, Jr.,* 1993) refers to the "classless" tradition of rural places with no local aristocracy. If you grew up respectable in a town like Double Springs, Alabama, you acknowledged no one above you, and there was no one below you who *knew* he was below you. In the interview with Bill Moyers, Johnson summed up the small-town point of view: "People in my section of the country have a fiercely independent attitude and personality. They have an intense respect for the individual and the individual's right. They believe in a person's dignity, and they believe each person is possessed of and is entitled to integrity. They believe that without regard to race, creed, color or ideology. 'Every man's his own man' is a real basic philosophy."

Johnson is usually described as fearless, but stubborn was the word his friends used. Neither the stick nor the carrot will move the kind of mule they breed in Winston County. Segregationists never understood how much their cause was damaged when racist thugs burned a cross on Johnson's lawn, and firebombed his mother's house; Montgomery society never understood how little he cared for country club memberships or invitations to black-tie balls. Judge Johnson's recollection of one such occasion is a cracker-barrel classic: "Went to one. These men 65 or 70 years old with white gloves and all that sort of stuff. Some of them with monkey suits on. Doing a lot of drinking. Late in the evening challenging each other to a duel. Ruth said I talked too loud. Biggest bunch of bullshit I've ever seen."

His lone-wolf Winston ways—deploring injustice but doubting the government's ability to set it right—often placed Johnson at odds with the consensus-building, bureaucracy-trusting Northern Democrats who came to save Alabama in the '60s. Frank Johnson was not your man to join hands and sing the anthems of Odetta and Joan Baez.

His decisions desegregating Alabama's schools, buses, and voting booths (and humanizing its prisons and mental institutions) were never motivated by a liberal, bleeding-heart ideology—only by what he perceived to be fair, reasonable, legal, and part of his jurisdiction. He outraged civil rights activists with some of his rulings, and once threatened to "put some Klansmen, some policemen, and some Negro preachers" in Atlanta penitentiary side by side.

He'd have been wounded if he thought most of his mourners would be Yankees. A tobacco-chewing, bass-fishing, George B. Dickel-drinking country lawyer, Frank Johnson was Alabama to the bone. Hell, his mother was named Alabama—Alabama Long. Of all the abuse Johnson suffered, none was more unjust than the yellow-journalists' assertion that he was an unnatural native son, an alien creature of Northern institutions and Northern conspiracies. "Carpetbagger" was the least of the epithets visited on Judge Johnson by George Wallace, who once suggested that he could benefit from "a barbed-wire enema."

"You work for Frank Johnson?" a Montgomery butcher asked one of Johnson's law clerks. "When he dies, people are going to line up to piss on his grave"—a queue that never materialized.

Dixie's diehards are glacially slow to forgive Southerners who stood up for different principles, in 1860 or 1960, and saw those principles prevail. It will be a cold August in Birmingham when most Alabamans concede that Frank Johnson's ancestors were right about secession. Officially, they've already conceded that Johnson was right about segregation. In 1992 the federal courthouse in Montgomery was renamed in the judge's honor, and a bronze bust of Johnson was placed in the lobby.

It was more reconciliation than Frank Johnson expected or required. When George Wallace called to ask the Johnsons to forgive him, he was rebuffed. The judge had reached a decision that he refused to reverse on appeal, even for an old man in a wheelchair: "George sent me a message that he wanted forgiveness. I sent him a message back that if he wanted to get forgiveness, he'd have to get it from the Lord."

III

THE CROSS

Varieties of Religious
Experience

A Feast of Snakes

It was at a friend's wedding last summer in Southwest Virginia, up in Tazewell County. One of the out-of-town guests—an architect from LA—wanted to take a walk up the mountainside, but he was worried about snakes.

"You have rattlesnakes in these mountains, don't you?"

"I don't know," I said, and I turned to my wife. "Honey, you were born and raised up here. Did you ever see any?"

"I never saw a rattlesnake in my life," she replied, "—except in church."

She cracked us up, of course, because she was just telling the truth and didn't realize how funny it was going to be until she got halfway into the punch line. You hate to confirm stereotypes for architects from LA. But it's hard to hide the culture gap between Southern California and the Southern Appalachians. Actually my wife worshiped with serpent handlers when she was researching a book, not when she was growing up in Buchanan County. One of her guides to the snake churches was a produce man in one of her cousin's grocery stores, who claims that serpent handling cured him of homosexuality and wearing dresses.

I think Doug Marlette gets credit for the line, "This town was so backward, even the Episcopalians handled snakes." Marlette's comic strip, *Kudzu,* is the only syndicated strip with God as a regular character and a flawed Baptist preacher, Reverend Will B. Dunn, as its guiding personality.

"The Lord works in strange ways," Reverend Dunn often reminds us. He doesn't need to remind us that the Lord works in stranger ways down South. How could my Unitarian parents prepare me for the woman who preaches on cable Channel 48? The screen is all dark and then a single spotlight finds her high up in a balcony, closer to heaven; she's short and her voice is soft as any angel's and her hair— Lord, her hair is gargantuan. I like big hair; my wife is not a woman of modest hair. But this person's hair has a life of its own. It has its own apartment.

I still can't hold a God-fearing, front-pew pokerface, even in my car, when I listen to the preacher on station WPIR in Hickory, North Carolina: "Satan is a-breathin' down your neck—ah-huh—He's a-grapplin' for your precious soul—ah-huh—The smell of the Pit is all around you—ah-huh—Will the Lord hear you when you holler?— ah-huh—Will you be cast into the lake of fire?—Uhhhh!"

His pneumatic version of the old-fashioned chanted sermon sounds like a boxer slamming the heavy bag at Singer's gym. When he finishes, the preacher's too used up to say "amen," and the announcer introduces a Christian singing group—the only three women in these music-rich mountains who are unable to carry a tune. They butcher a gospel standard. Then a high-voiced country woman starts preaching about the evil of computers, debit cards, and ATM machines, part of the Antichrist's plan to take over the world by eliminating money and locking up everything we own in the devil's database. "It's the Mark of the Beast on those little cards," she wails. "They're getting us used to the Darkness, little by little." (Actually this part is beginning to make a lot of sense to me.)

Someone said the Bible Belt likes its religion the same as its whiskey—strong, homemade, and none too subtle. A recent book by historian Christine Leigh Heyrman—*Southern Cross: The Beginnings of the Bible Belt*—argues that it wasn't always this way. For two hundred years, as Heyrman tells it, the South was a stronghold of easygoing Anglicans who produced—and tolerated—deists and doubters like Thomas Jefferson.

In Heyrman's scenario, hellfire evangelism and scriptural literalism crept down the Appalachians from the Northeast during the nineteenth-century migrations. They were never identified as distinctly Southern until H. L. Mencken published his devastating accounts of Tennessee's Scopes "monkey trial" in 1925. But like the kudzu, they were imports that found the red clay country more than congenial. You'll find no vestige of the Anglican, or the Enlightenment, in the Christianity of Billy Graham. The South's most influential clergyman, by virtue of pulpit power and personal integrity, Graham is a former Fuller Brush salesman who baits his hook with as little theology as any of God's fishermen.

Graham is all faith and no filigree. His simple message, "Just give yourself to Christ," probably made things easier for the abominable Jim Bakker, whose message was "Just give your money to Jim." Bakker's miracle was his credibility with so many trusting souls. The first time I saw Jim and Tammy Faye, I swear I thought they were two male comics from Long Island doing a brilliant sendup of televangelism. Jim looked like a laboratory gerbil some sadist had overdosed with amphetamines; Tammy Faye sang like Tiny Tim and looked like a bad Jackson Pollock drying slowly. Some people thought they had the keys to the Kingdom of God.

If the word "Jesus" functions as a license to steal, maybe it should be a controlled substance in the South, illegal in most situations, the way it should be illegal for men to use the word "love" on lonely women.

Face it, we have a regional weakness for this stuff. I married a brilliant woman who used to haunt revival tents when she was a kid, who was saved so many times she embarrassed her parents and got sent away to school in Richmond, where they hoped the Bible-thumpers couldn't find her. She used to come home dripping wet from total immersion.

That's no reason to be defensive. There are single neighborhoods in California that have spawned more religions—in the past twenty years—than have ever been practiced in the South. At least in the South most people worship God, not L. Ron Hubbard or some psycho with a crewcut who channels for Jeremiah.

The Heaven's Gate necronauts didn't take off from Hickory. We don't need to apologize for our churches—though a little humility is appropriate. Too many white churches played no role, or a negative one, in the moral revolution that overthrew Jim Crow. Separate-but-equal salvation has to rank as one of the most dubious achievements that ever dishonored Jesus Christ.

In an interview in Susan Ketchin's *The Christ-Haunted Landscape,* novelist Doris Betts describes the mystery of racist Christians: "There's just a hole in many Southerners. There's just a hole. You can walk right up to it and fall in. It's like the San Andreas fault." But that fault is closing, Betts believes. The most dangerous thing about That Old Time Religion may turn out to be its contempt for doubt. Strong, inflexible beliefs can be a great help to an individual. But when too many people hold them in common, almost invariably they get to believing that everyone should hold them. Some of us hate evangelism for its attitude, not its message. How do I explain to Billy Graham, a good man, why pitching his gospel to me is like trying to sell binoculars to Stevie Wonder?

A little doubt is sane and normal. Watch out for the guy who has none. Bolt your doors if he says he's a prophet. It filled me with profound misgivings to read that Pat Robertson was out of his box again, exhorting businessmen to join him in destroying the godless Democrats in the year 2000.

This millennium means a little more to Robertson than it means to you or me. He published a book about the Apocalypse, a work of "Christian fiction" titled *The End of the Age.* The End begins in 1995 and climaxes with the Battle of Armageddon and the Second Coming of Christ (in a giant spaceship, "a jeweled cube fourteen hundred miles on each side")—in the year 2000.

Robertson's Antichrist turns out to be an American president, a secret radical and heir to Wall Street billions (Steve Forbes?).

At the 1988 Republican Convention, only George Bush and Bob Dole polled more delegates than this modest author. If you think constitutional democracy is important enough to have its own Antichrist, Pat Robertson is my nominee. He believes that he can heal the sick and that his prayers kept Hurricane Gloria from destroying Virginia Beach.

Jefferson had good reason for separating church and state. If you think you're doing what God demands, why should you care what anyone else thinks? No one man can erase two hundred years of civil liberties, but Pat Robertson may be the only man who would try.

A snake-handling woman told my wife she took up serpents "out of an intense desire for holiness." But it's in the shadow of this beautiful desire, which can free us from reasonable doubt, that a snake can grow too big for anyone to handle.

Angels on the Interstate

At times the hostages, terrorists, and dead and dying movie stars make such a noise in the world that you can't hear yourself hum over it. If you have some reason other than curiosity to listen—like making a living—it can be deafening. At those times you have to retreat to something that actually *is* in its own right, to counteract these distorted images of distant, ambiguous things that the media present for our amazement and their enrichment.

When it happens to me, I revert to the one kind of irresponsible behavior, out of many kinds that my mother deplored, that in sober manhood I've never fully abandoned. I take enormous long drives, often at night, sometimes in the rain and fog, sometimes even without my seatbelt fastened. Always when there are serious things I should be doing and considering instead. I drive too fast. I drive the way I imagine a trucker drives, the captain of an eighteen-wheeler, not so much sightseeing or philosophizing but appreciating the feeling of eating up the distance, of chewing up and spitting out the miles. When I was younger I could drive for almost twenty-four hours without stopping for more than five minutes at a time. I'm under fifteen hours, now, before life-threatening exhaustion sets in, but I can still run off eight or ten as easily as most people drive to work.

On these long runs, in a trucker's trance, you see everything with a kind of peripheral vision, out of the corner of your eye into the corner of your brain. You see a lot but don't react much, at least not immediately. Last week I started out at Abingdon, in the far Wild West of Virginia, and drove all the way up the spine of the Appalachians to

Corning, New York. A total of 645 miles, driving time eleven hours counting all necessary stops. If you could compare driving to running it would be something like a half marathon by a fairly serious runner. Runners don't have to watch out for radar, but drivers don't have to watch out for cramps or dehydration.

Fall foliage was my excuse for the drive, the only excuse anyone else would understand. When the sun came up over the Virginia mountains, somewhere south of Roanoke, there were some red maples that almost exploded, like torches soaked in kerosene. The gorge where Route 81 crosses Buffalo Creek was spectacular, the brightest color I saw south of Pennsylvania. But the clouds spread quickly and most of the day was damp and overcast, and the colors muted. The story of my life, it would be very much like me to say—six hundred miles of drizzle and disappointment.

But I didn't really go to see the leaves. I was in need of something actual and familiar, a stretch of world I knew well enough to make comparisons between the past and present. I've been driving in those mountains most of my life. But the last time I drove so far I was twenty-four, on my way to New Orleans (driving time twenty-one hours, thirty minutes). I remember shacks along the ridges with the sunset behind them, a notion of being free of everything, all those Lost in America emotions that William Least Heat-Moon recorded in *Blue Highways.* I didn't keep a journal, but I wrote a long third-rate poem about leaving pieces of myself in every state along the way until I hit Louisiana picked clean and "light as a dirigible." In an airplane distances don't treat you like that, they don't force you to leave anything along the way.

Route 81. The night before I heard a writer say that there used to be panthers on these mountaintops. The panthers are gone, along with half of the trees where they used to hide out. But it's still fairly wild up there. The further you get from the cities, the more animals you see mangled on the highways. Where the traffic is light the animals are less sophisticated, and there's a horrible harvest of road meat. Even dogs. You won't see a dead dog on the Washington Beltway. Either there are no strays, or no stupid animals left alive. But up in the mountains three of them wandered in front of my mile-hungry Mazda, high beams and all, as if it was no more threatening than a milk cow. After I missed one by a whisker, with the help of a horn blast that bruised my hand, he drifted back into the passing lane behind me and sat down on the yellow line. In heavy ground fog near Gettysburg, a trucker just ahead of me hit a deer at full speed, with no chance to brake or swerve if he wanted to. The highway looked like a butcher shop for buzzards.

If there were any panthers left when they built these highways, they didn't last long. But up in those Virginia hills you can still hear strange creatures screaming in the night. Turn your radio dial to WWVA, Wheeling, West Virginia. This powerful station, which carries all over the mountains and must reach fifteen states at night, features a lineup of evangelists on cassettes.

In the mountains, in the dark, five hundred miles from home, a long-haul driver will give any messenger a fair hearing. The radio evangelists are no strangers to anyone who grew up in the Appalachians. When I was a boy with a learner's permit, this same station had a giveaway of long standing, a free ($2 for shipping and handling?) rolling pin bearing the inscription "I am the bread of life." But what was only quaint in those days, a droll lesson in strange doctrines for my family of Unitarians and agnostics, this same harmless chorus of charlatans has been hardened into something so shrill and fierce that it freezes the traveler's spirit and turns his mind to wolves.

It may be the driver who has changed. But more likely it's the competition, the slick television preachers with the media manners and the million-dollar budgets, which has skimmed off the fat of the land and driven these hungry old predators to howl so fiercely from their last few transmitters in these changeless mountains.

The cassettes are repeated in sequence, so that each act on the bill gets a second and a third chance at the thin wallets of the hardscrabble farmers and laid-off miners' wives who must make up most of the radio audience. Plain flat-voiced fools are a welcome relief. The

only preacher I heard with a trace of humility was selling old-fashioned Bible prophecy, and sounding unconvinced himself. Was the
Antichrist going to be Judas Iscariot resurrected (a foolish heresy, he
decided) or was it Henry Kissinger? Kissinger, he said, is a candidate
to be watched—a smooth diplomat without scruples who will, in the
final days before Armageddon, bring about a symbolic seven-year
truce between the Arabs and the Jews.

The strangest of all was a fifteen-minute cassette featuring Brother
Onesimus, a white man with a New York accent, and Brother Bar-Bar
Judah IV (or something close to that), a black man with a pulse rate
of eleven or twelve and a voice like an anaesthetized James Earl Jones.
Their appeal seemed to drift from fundamentalism into some kind of
mysticism that I couldn't begin to decipher, in three hearings. Brother
Bar-Bar repeated the phrase "The I Am" like a mantra, two or three
helpings of it to a sentence, ten to a paragraph. "We wait in The I
Am, we exist in The I Am, we are at rest in The I Am, and at length
the The I Am will whisper 'You are.'" The Tower of Babel loomed
above my Mazda. Of all the utter nonsense that has been uttered
since the dawn of speech, I wrote somewhere, nine-tenths has been uttered into microphones in rural America in the past thirty years, in the
name of Jesus Christ.

It was a brief respite from The Howling. "Why are your children
rotten?" screamed one old man with the full voice of a senator.
"They're rotten because you feed them rotten food." The decibel level
rose and rose as "full Gospel" preachers condemned charismatics,
total immersionists condemned dry-look city Baptists, the twice-born
condemned the once-born, and everyone condemned rock and roll.
Sister Yvonne, who comes to us with an ancient father named Dr.
Douglas, interrupts "Dad" to explain something called backward
masking, a technique used by record companies and rock groups to
promote Satan, drug abuse, and "unusual sexual practices." Buy the
book—the money is needed for missions and orphanages. And please
remember us in your will.

The crescendo is Brother Shambach, defying Satan with a harsh, starving voice strained to the shattering point, a voice that finally dies to a hoarse whisper, but a whisper that nevertheless conveys the critical post office box number with astonishing clarity. After three hours of it I turn the dial on my radio. Sometimes Grace is nearest when it seems most far away. I get Emmylou Harris, singing something old and true in that sweet clear voice with just a touch of whiskey in it, that raw touch that makes it country and makes it great. And it's a blessing to me, as Brother Shambach always says but never was. Does he, do any of them recognize an angel's voice when they hear one?

The Hounds of Heaven

Every newspaper in the country picked up the story. A ten-year-old boy with Down's Syndrome was lost in the Ozark Mountains for three nights, in subfreezing March temperatures. The child was rescued in remarkably good condition, except for some frostbitten toes, and his survival was credited to a pair of stray dogs who kept him warm with their bodies and attracted the search party with their barking. The boy's stepfather, who adopted the strays, called them "God's angels."

Joe Murray, a worthwhile newspaperman from Lufkin, Texas, was inspired to write a column about some friends of his who were lost in similar rough country—and led back to the road by two mysterious white dogs.

"It would be wonderful to arrive in Heaven and find that angels are dogs," Murray wrote, "and that the dogs we had in our life on Earth had been our guardian angels."

Nice, Joe. How many newspaper columns leave us with lumps in our throats? And the idea of dogs with celestial pedigrees is catching on. In "The White Dogs," North Carolina poet Tony Abbott pictures two white Salukis—sacred dogs of ancient Egypt—who wait at the door of a Blue Ridge cabin to carry off the soul of his dying friend.

Another lump, there. I can't even read *Dog Music,* a collection of poems my wife bought me for my birthday, because I skipped through and got the impression that half of them are about dogs dying. I'm learning to cry, and I appreciate an opportunity on occasion, but I just don't have the time to sit up in my room and blubber.

If this is a weakness, it's one I share with some pretty tough customers. Take Louis-Ferdinand Celine, an anti-Semite convicted of collaborating with the Nazis, a tortured cynic who wrote novels that bare their teeth at the human race and never stop snarling. Celine saw no innocence in the world, and little virtue. But dogs impressed and moved him deeply—especially their deaths. The death of his dog Bessy inspired this passage in *Castle to Castle,* the best glimpse of his heart Celine ever gave us:

> I held her in my arms up to the end . . . really a splendid animal
> . . . a joy to look at her . . . a vibrant joy . . . she was so beautiful!
> Oh, I've seen plenty of death agonies . . . here . . . there . . . everywhere . . . but none by far so beautiful, so discreet . . . so faithful. The trouble with men's death agonies is the song and dance . . . a man is always on the stage . . . even the simplest of them.

Faulkner understood perfectly. No passage in *The Bear* captures its spirit like the death of Lion, the fearless dog who matched and doomed the bear, Old Ben: "there were almost a hundred of them squatting and standing in the warm and drowsing sunlight, talking quietly of hunting, of the game and the dogs which ran it, of hounds and bear and deer and men of yesterday vanished from the earth, while from time to time the great blue dog would open his eyes, not as if he were listening to them but as though to look at the woods for a moment before closing his eyes again, to remember the woods or to see that they were still there. He died at sundown."

They still appreciate dogs in Mississippi. In two recent Mississippi memoirs—*On Fire* by Larry Brown and *My Dog Skip* by Willie Morris—the death of a favorite dog is the most painful thing the author can remember. There's no false stoicism, either, no tough-guys-don't-cry stuff to insulate the reader from the pain.

"Die like a dog" is a pejorative simile that turns up in action literature of a certain vintage. It was invented by a miserable observer. We should all aspire to die so well, with a dog's solemn dignity that shames all our sweaty confessions and crucifix-clutching, our the-

atrics. If dogs are angels, they know they're saved; if they're dumb innocent creatures, death is one more uncomfortable feeling that comes
over them, like hunger or sexual heat. Either way we admire their
composure, and envy it profoundly.

The worth of dogs goes unquestioned in the best Southern literature. In the fiction of Cormac McCarthy (beginning with *The Orchard Keeper* in 1965, most recently in the last scene of *The Crossing*
in 1994) a sin against a dog is a paradigm of evil and moral failure.

Dogs elicit maudlin testimonials from the most unlikely sources.
I'm one of them. I can't match McCarthy's pessimism or Celine's mis-
anthropy, but no one ever confused me with Norman Rockwell or
Norman Vincent Peale. I've yet to shed a tear at a wedding or a patriotic demonstration, and babies, with the exception of my own,
never made much of an impression on me. Bad movies with emotional sucker-punches rarely hit me at all—unless something ugly
happens to a dog.

People who reproach us for loving animals more than people are
usually hypocrites who love neither. No individual incapable of baby-
talking to an Airedale would ever be among my closest friends. And
the very lowest rungs on my personal ladder of life are occupied by
people who've mistreated a dog, betrayed a dog who loved them or
even failed to love a dog who deserved it.

These prejudices are the product of experience, unaffected by any
notion that I'm a red-blooded, wing-shooting, *Field & Stream* sort
of dog-man who kicks his wife's cats. Butch, my yellow tomcat, slept
under my left arm every night for fifteen years, and I wouldn't have
traded him for a saddle horse. The bad blood between cat people and
dog people is as phony, in my view, as animosities between universities that compete in sports.

The truth is that anyone capable of appreciating one admirable
animal can appreciate another. Hating cats is an irrational prejudice,
much like anti-Semitism, that boys often pick up from their fathers.
It's a primitive canard that soft men love cats and hard men love dogs.
Honest men respond to both. Celine's beloved cat Bebert is a major
character in *Castle to Castle*. Willie Morris owned four cats.

I never had a dog all my own until I was over forty. Obviously this dog has made a great believer of me. If you asked me what sets dogs above and apart from other animals, I'd say it's a moral quality. Dogs are utterly unlike us, sharing none of our goals, preoccupations, or belief systems—as the poet Howard Nemerov observes in "Walking the Dog": "Two universes mosey down the street / Connected by love and a leash and nothing else."

And yet they involve themselves in our lives, in ways that can't be explained by simple affection or canine self-interest. I hate to brag on my own dog; I'm sure her virtues are common ones. Yet I watch her break up every fight among the house cats, at considerable inconvenience and even peril to herself. She stifles quarrels between her human housemates by banging to be let out, the second one of us reaches a decibel level she finds offensive. She shames us into civility.

Who appointed her peacekeeper? Call it altruism, a sense of duty, a commitment to domestic tranquility. Call it self-righteousness. But you won't get it from a parrot or a pot-bellied pig.

The moral superiority of dogs is an easy case to argue. They come in all temperaments, from Lion who according to Faulkner "cared about no man and no thing" to my Lab, Gracie, who appears to love every man and every living thing she encounters. But whereas human beings are continually blasting each other to pieces over traffic disputes or trivial pieces of property, I've never seen another dog fail to respond in kind to my dog's flawless amiability—unless you count this one thing so small and ugly it might have been a fuzzy rodent doing a poor impersonation of a dog.

If you condescend to dogs because they eat things we hate to step in, and resort to grooming tricks we find outré, you've mistaken your affected pantywaist hygiene for moral and intellectual superiority. There are almost no limits to a dog's potential except the ones humans have carelessly bred or trained or beaten into him.

Another poet, Lord Byron, wrote this epitaph for his Newfoundland, Boatswain: "One who possessed beauty without vanity, strength without insolence, courage without ferocity, and all the virtues of man without his vices."

It takes more than the testimony of poets to prove that dogs are angels. But anecdotal evidence is piling up. The same week the boy was rescued in the Ozarks, an Irish setter was credited with saving her owner's life by dialing 911. And a big Lab/Rottweiler mix stopped traffic—stood in the road—to get help for a boy who had fainted from insulin shock.

Next to Interstate 95 near Lumberton, North Carolina, is a billboard with a dog's picture and these words: "This dog saved my daughter's life. Now he's lost. 'Spook'—$3,500 reward." Considering all the sad things that may have happened to Spook, we comfort ourselves with the possibility that he simply completed his mission, and was reassigned.

Through twelve thousand years of intimate association, humans have been a mixed blessing for their patient guardians. Lofty moral examples often provoke lethal reprisals, as Jesus, Socrates, or Gandhi could testify. (A news item from High Point, North Carolina: A dog-fighting ring dumps a load of dead and maimed animals by the side of the road. One dead dog has part of its jaw missing, another has no legs.)

How can dogs square their noble mission with some of the savage treatment they receive in return?

I remember the answer, from the fantasy comic strip *Barbarella*, which became a Jane Fonda movie. One of the characters is an angel. Barbarella asks him why he's rescuing a villain who crucified him in an earlier episode, and he replies, "Angels have no memory."

The King and I

The King works in strange ways. I reached the age of forty without thinking of Elvis Presley much at all, maybe less than any American who witnessed his entire reign and could boast, if grandchildren ever asked me, "Yes, I saw Elvis—live."

It all made so little impression that I was married to a woman for years and never realized, until after the divorce, that she had the same birthday as The King. Elvis was long dead when I married again and discovered that my Southern-fried bride came equipped with a curious religious relic—a dried red carnation from one of the floral arrangements pilgrims heaped on Presley's coffin at Graceland. My wife plucked it herself and had it framed, over a postcard painting of Elvis in his prime.

That was just the beginning. I'm not a superstitious man, one who records coincidences with an eye to divine intentions. But judge for yourself. In the years since I first became aware of the Elvis cult, I've acquired some unusual friends.

One has authored two Elvis books, the most recent an account of his adventures as a middle-aged Elvis impersonator (*I, Elvis* by William McCranor Henderson, 1997). He got into impersonation as a kick, to honor a book contract, and now I think he's hooked. He makes appearances in a big slick ducktail wig and a white body-suit, and throws salmon-colored scarves at the audience.

Another friend has become Elvis Presley's most respected biographer. The first volume of his two-part life of Presley was published in 1994 (*Last Train to Memphis* by Peter Guralnick), and he's widely recognized as The Leading Authority, period. Yet another, the versatile Fetzer Mills, actually landed a job on the security force at Graceland and gave us the VIP tour in his EPD (Elvis Police Department) uniform. Last Christmas he sent us a cassette of him singing his rockabilly favorites, backed by the Memphis session musicians who cut those first Sun records with Elvis.

These are not casual connections of mine but actual friends, the kind who might offer to adopt your dogs if you died. My wife, of course, takes it for granted that life will bring you into contact with a lot of people who dress like Elvis or write about him. To me it's uncanny, like turning my radio dial and hearing "Love Me Tender" on every bleeding station.

Elvis, departed and risen, keeps after me as he never did in life. I feel like the loser who was invited to the Crucifixion but stayed home to mend his nets, or whatever Galileans did on weekends. I was around, I could have been there. But I just didn't get it.

Have you noticed how in *Ben-Hur,* and all Hollywood's action epics in-the-time-of-Christ, the important thing is always happening off-camera, or just at the edge of the frame? Charlton Heston or Victor Mature or Richard Burton is going about his very butch business of racing chariots, subduing Nubia or selling slaves, and he keeps passing these crowds of people whose faces are all shining with an inner light, who have just come from hearing The Master. ("Why are you smiling, boy?" "I have heard Him, sir.")

I feel like a self-absorbed centurion who was preoccupied, marching to another drumbeat while the Main Event of his lifetime occurred just across the road. Did I miss the main thing, too, and was it Elvis?

As a kid I was an uncomprehending witness. I saw Elvis's first national TV performance on the Dorsey Brothers' show, one of my father's favorite programs. I saw the famous Ed Sullivan debut. The music was OK, but a sexual and racial breakthrough? I was a child. How could I comprehend that I was witnessing the birth of a world religion?

Later, we had nothing in common, Elvis and I. Since all my repression was self-generated, I couldn't see Elvis as a liberator. I didn't worry that greasers like Elvis were getting all the sex, because I wasn't getting much anyway.

A class thing separated us, as well as a city/country thing. I was a teacher's son, deep country but not cool country. I knew only one boy who greased his hair creatively. He was a city kid, living with foster parents, who called himself Tony Price (a great name, but in class the teachers called him David Eck). Tony was authentically tough, much tougher than Elvis from what I've read. Ultimately he kicked Bill Hamilton in the crotch with his motorcycle boot and sent Bill to the hospital with bloody urine; the principal expelled Tony, and his foster parents sent him back to the agency.

It never occurred to me to emulate Tony, or Elvis either. Maybe I fit the standard profile of the teenager who missed the point of the '50s, if the point was Elvis and Brando, James Dean and Jack Kerouac. Elvis never seemed dangerous, to me. If I'd heard Greil Marcus's argument—that the mainstream press made Presley a scapegoat because Yankee middlebrows just naturally fear, despise, and stereotype the Southern working class (a vendetta culminating with *Elvis,* Albert Goldman's merciless biography)—I might have adopted Elvis as an underdog.

Challenging authority was not my hangup. From underage drinking to light vandalism to dissing teachers, I practiced most of the bad attitude in the adolescent repertoire, back before drugs hit the schools. Just convict me of a hopeless, middle-class failure of imagination. I tried to dress like a college kid, and wore my hair in a hideous semiflattop.

The music scene, like the dating scene, came to me ever so slowly. I didn't dance if I could avoid it. I was tall and shy, and I had some white-boy problems with the way rhythms traveled from my brain to my feet. I hated to see rock 'n' roll replace slow dancing because I sweated so fiercely; any girl who tried to Twist within three feet of me would have to change her clothes. Ten minutes on the dance floor and I looked like I'd worked a night shift on a banana barge.

The first wave of Elvis idolaters were thinking with their glands and with their feet. If you missed that first wave, the second one required some musical sophistication. Presley's comeback TV special in 1968 included a rockabilly blues segment that Greil Marcus calls "the most mature and passionate music Elvis ever made." But Elvis was not what was happening, in 1968. When it comes to cultural prescience, I didn't handle the '60s much better than the '50s. I was working in my office in the Time-Life building when three of my friends tried to recruit me for the long drive up to Woodstock. I'd just watched the awful traffic jams on TV, and I declined emphatically.

When I finally caught up to Elvis—in his earthly incarnation—he was forty years old and stumbling to his own pharmaceutical crucifixion. It was July 13, 1975, at the Niagara Falls Convention Center. The songs were achingly familiar. They moved us because we were thirty, the age when nostalgia first strikes. We beheld The King Himself, a legend just slightly smaller, at that time, than Dylan or the Beatles.

It had to be Elvis, because an impersonator would have looked more authentic. The singer was swollen; someone in the next row said he was wearing a corset. Through our binoculars it appeared that his chest fat was pushed up into the V of his shirt, like a little ascot made of flesh. His voice was hoarse and his body language, to put it kindly, had lost its eloquence.

Elvis live was not a conversion experience; Elvis dead became a pathetic tabloid mutation that forced me to sneer. On the tenth anniversary of The Death, in 1987, I wrote a column deploring the Graceland Cult as the state religion of the degenerate "voodoo republic" that's replacing Mr. Jefferson's dignified democracy. I added gratuitously that poor Elvis, without the testosterone growl in his larynx and the feral curl in his lip, would have made his living as a forklift operator.

But mysteriously, unmistakably, my tone has softened. A decade later, in a column on Elvis and Mickey Mantle—America's twin gods for the sweet lost summer of 1956—I hear myself testifying for the defense: "Can you make a grown man or woman cry over the way you looked, the way you moved, forty years ago? . . . We love them because they were, for a shining moment, something bigger and finer than most of us ever dreamed of being."

But pilgrims don't kneel in the cold rain at Mickey Mantle's tomb. Or at the tomb of Carl Perkins, who wrote and first recorded "Blue Suede Shoes." Perkins died still explaining why his career fell so far short of the King's: "I was bucking a good-looking cat called Elvis who had beautiful hair, wasn't married, and had all kinds of great moves."

The question of why they're still crying in the chapel—why one icon explodes like a nova while all the others fade—may be a debate for theologians of the twenty-second century, when a guitar crowns those steeples that once held up the cross.

I can only bear personal witness. No one ever tried to convince or convert me. Like those Christians Charlton Heston kept meeting on his way to the Forum, Presley's disciples proselytize with their own serenity and conviction. If you need to explain it, they imply, you haven't got it.

I walk through my own house, and there's no sign that people raised as Christians live here. But the funeral carnation from Graceland still sits on the mantel; from the windowsill, a wooden cutout Elvis sneers at me over his shoulder. On the kitchen corkboard my wife has pinned the salmon scarf from a performance by our friend Bill, in his wig and sequined bodysuit.

Above it is the Elvis clock, the same one you see in millions of American homes, with Elvis' blue-and-white-checked trouser legs for a pendulum. The best symbol for our poor mortal lives is the sand running through the hourglass. But Elvis *keeps* time; he's waiting, and he has all the time in the world.

Cross Purposes

The most democratic feature of the fully armed society is that it opens up the front page and the evening news to everyone. Nothing satiates the media's hunger for violent possibilities, and no American is so humble, despised, or disadvantaged that a little firepower can't elevate him to instant celebrity.

I think of that when I go out for coffee, very early in the morning, and spy some of the night people crawling off to their holes—timid, medicated people who look like lemurs with dark rings around eyes that never blink. Any one of them could be in next week's headlines, like Wendell Williamson who strolled down that same street in Chapel Hill shooting students off their bicycles with an M-1 rifle from World War II. He had stopped taking his medication, the newspapers reported.

America will never see another civil war, but anyone overwhelmed and overlooked—or just undermedicated and confused—can stage his own version of an armed revolution. Theodore Kaczynski and Timothy McVeigh were lemur-people, nocturnal hunters, lonely theorists who came to apocalyptic conclusions.

Only the weakest among them join tribes. When the FBI smoked the Freemen out of their nest in Montana, the prisoners made a little parade for the media and even newswire reporters described them with contempt: outcasts, deadbeats, damaged refugees from misogynist cults and incestuous families—fugitives from reality who were chronically out of work, out of touch, out of luck. The theorist and spokesman for this group, a certain Skurdal, is a former White House security officer who suffered a serious head injury and "has difficulty making appropriate connections."

A ragged army of rejects, addled and dispossessed, drawn from the dregs of a white underclass that defines itself with racist theory and armed paranoia. Under what banner would such a rabble fight? When the Freemen surrendered, they raised an upside-down American flag, a signal of distress. And then they replaced it with a Confederate battle flag.

Rest in peace, Robert E. Lee. There was a time when underdogs weren't so mangy. The flag of the Confederacy, the Southern Cross, has been much abused and dishonored since Lee laid it down— saluted by night riders, flown in defiance of voting rights and integration, fastened to the bumpers of rusty pickups filled with church-bombers and killers. It remains a source of controversy because it will always mean different things to different Americans. To Yankees, stubbornness and sour grapes; to blacks, a palpable threat; to many honorable Southerners, courage, sacrifice, and an inalienable right to their own history.

Over some fierce and understandable objections, I've always defended the use of this flag, as long as the people who use it are honest about their motives and comfortable with them. I'm afraid I can't abide the leftist attack on the First Amendment, the one that runs, "You can't say that, you can't wear that, you can't show that or play that because it hurts my feelings, never mind about your feelings."

The Southern Cross and the lost cause that still honors it have had enough to bear, without the Freemen. But symbols are in the public domain. They don't choose their friends or control their associations. Coca-Cola ran its Olympic torches through a thousand villages, including mine, where a big crowd gathered to watch the torch go by. There were lots of children, ice cream cones, cameras, flags. A real all-American holiday atmosphere. I couldn't help wondering how many of my neighbors knew where this inspirational symbol originated. I guess most people think it goes back to Pheidippides or *The Iliad* or something Greek.

Actually it goes back to Adolf Hitler, or at least to his stage man-
ager Dr. Carl Diem, who came up with the torch as a symbol for the
Berlin Olympics in 1936. The Olympic flame has an ancient pedigree.
According to tradition, a flame burned on the altar of Zeus for the du-
ration of the first Olympic Games in Greece, in 776 B.C. The Dutch
revived the flame for the Amsterdam games in 1928. But the idea of
relay runners carrying the torch from Olympia to Berlin was pure
Nazi inspiration, though you won't read much about it now that the
torch has been passed to Coca-Cola.

The Nazis, masters of public theater and iconography, left bloody
fingerprints on some of the finest symbols in the business. In the area
of symbolism a short memory can be very convenient. If you own a
Mercedes-Benz or covet one, the Mercedes hood ornament (another
cross) symbolizes luxury, quality, and superior engineering. But it
stood for something quite different to the Poles of Warsaw when the
Führer's Mercedes prowled in triumph through their streets, and that
hood ornament, flanked by the swastika Führer-flag, led the whole
parade.

The swastika itself, one of the most ancient and amiable of all
symbols honored by the tribes of man, may never recover from its
heady run with Hitler. Its name, from Sanskrit, means "well-being."
Sacred to Buddhists, Hindus, Incas, Egyptians, Etruscans, and ancient cultures on every inhabited continent, the swastika in various
mythologies represented the sun, infinity, fire, creation, and rebirth.
It was always a symbol of good fortune—of prosperity, fertility, long
life, and divine protection.

The Nazis, whose mythology was no less muddled than their
genetics, embraced the swastika as an emblem of Aryan supremacy.
According to *Mein Kampf,* it symbolizes "the fight for victory of
Aryan man and of the idea of creative work, which in itself eternally
has been anti-Semitic and eternally will be anti-Semitic."

The swastika was never seen much in the South, not until recently
when Klansmen and Nazi skinheads discovered each other's charms.
But in its pre-Führer innocence it greeted Mississippi River travelers

from the flagstaffs of the Memphis Power Boat Club. I discovered the club's pennant with its counterclockwise swastika in a color illustration from a 1913 dictionary. It wasn't a lucky emblem for the MPBC, long defunct. So far no one in Memphis has been able to tell me when it folded or whether it changed its colors to acknowledge the sinking fortunes of the swastika.

Unsavory associations are a curse the swastika or gamma cross shares with its younger brother, the cross of Jesus Christ. The burning crosses of the Ku Klux Klan were only a footnote to a long history of bloodshed and intolerance, of murder and atrocity conducted under the auspices of the cross. The cross loomed over the Inquisition, the massacres and pogroms conducted by the crusaders, the centuries of bloody warfare between Catholics and Protestants. It stood for authority when they burned Joan of Arc, Jan Hus, and Jacques de Molay, the Grand Master of the Knights Templar, along with legions of nameless "heretics" and "witches" whose souls were purified in the flames.

The church of the cross has regained some of its luster in the twentieth century, and the conservative Pope John Paul has earned respect (seasoned with irony) by going around apologizing for the mortal sins of his predecessors. But in the eighteenth century crosses bore such ambivalent associations that apostles of the Enlightenment would generally steer clear of them. Those apostles included most of the Founding Fathers of the United States of America.

The politics of the religious Right rest on its assertion that the United States was founded as a Christian nation. It's more accurate to say that it was founded as a Deist nation, reflecting the ideals of Enlightenment *philosophes* and Freemasons who thought too much religion had made a cruel mess of Europe.

Some of the great geniuses of the eighteenth century—Voltaire, Goethe, Mozart—were Masonic initiates. The Masons were unpopular with kings and especially odious to the Catholic Church because they practiced religious tolerance and kept the secrets of their order from clergymen and magistrates. You don't hear much about the Masons anymore, either as a force or a secret threat. But America's genesis makes no sense if you don't understand their influence.

Beginning with John Hancock, nine signers of the Declaration of Independence and thirteen signers of the Constitution were Masons. Proof of their power is as close as the dollar bill in your wallet. On one side there's George Washington, Master of a Masonic lodge in Alexandria, Virginia. Turn it over and you find the Great Seal of the United States, an intricate allegory of Masonic symbols playing off the number thirteen, which according to the late mythmaster Joseph Campbell is "the number of resurrection, of transformation and rebirth."

The Great Seal is a Masonic device that pays tribute to Judaism; note the Star of David above the eagle's head. But the cross is nowhere to be found, unless you insist on the word "one" which forms a crossbar for the number "1" in each corner.

Christians rest their claim on the motto "In God We Trust." But Campbell explains that the most dramatic Masonic symbol, the pyramid with the great eye at the top, represents "the mind of God," God inseparable from Reason—that nemesis of fundamentalists and Freemen everywhere.

If Pat Robertson could line up the Founding Fathers and ask each of them to make his choice between Faith and Reason, he might be crushed by the vote. Masons like Washington and Freethinkers like Thomas Jefferson, whose enemies attacked him as an atheist and Antichrist, hoped that Reason would free America of conflicting religious passions and guide it to the greatness they envisioned.

Lots of luck. The Founders' symbols faded along with their principles. Not long before Joseph Campbell's death in 1987, Bill Moyers asked him if he could predict the next generation of symbols that would replace the old ones we've exhausted and misused.

"Weapons, of course," said Campbell, years before the first Freeman made an appearance. "Every movie I see shows people with revolvers. There is the Lord Death, carrying his weapon."

You Are My Sunshine

Prominent on any short list of indelible cultural stereotypes is the Southern Belle, a fabulous creature whose sultry glamour was ever irresistible to America's innocent imagination. No culture type—no robber baron, riverboat gambler, Indian scout—has continued to reproduce itself with more fidelity to the original. Motion pictures, created in most cases by Yankees or foreigners, established her immortality. When a small town in the South dresses its young ladies for a beauty pageant or centennial celebration, its model is England's Vivien Leigh in *Gone With the Wind* or New England's Bette Davis in *Jezebel.* Belles have been stock film characters from the very beginning, when D. W. Griffith of Kentucky fashioned his imaginary South of lilywhite virgins and gallant Klansmen in *Birth of a Nation.*

Psychologically, movie belles range from frail fainting things in crinolines to the insufferable Scarlett O'Hara (described by Fred Chappell as "J.E.B. Stuart in drag") to even more frightening hearts masked by floral scents and lacy ballgowns—hearts Pat Conroy contemplates when he writes "the sweetness of Southern women often conceals the deadliness of snakes." Yet these lovely, unfathomable creatures—and this was the source of their fascination—all look the same from the far side of the ballroom.

You can close your eyes and see her, the ribbons on her shoulders and the curls behind her ears. But away from movie posters and ladies' magazines, where does the immortal icon meet the flesh-and-blood reality of women who live and die in Dixie? It's a field of debate that's been well plowed indeed, and some of the deepest furrows have been left by friends of mine.

I open the authoritative *Encyclopedia of Southern Culture* and I see that the entry on "Belles and Ladies" was written by my dear friend Anne Goodwyn Jones, a distinguished feminist scholar at the University of Florida. You wouldn't expect the belle to fare well from a feminist perspective; the essay amounts to a hostile deconstruction of what Jones, a North Carolina native, views as a pernicious, reactionary ideal.

"Southern womanhood has from the beginning been inextricably linked to racial attitudes," Jones writes. "In general, [historians] agree that the function of Southern womanhood has been to justify the perpetuation of the hegemony of the male sex, the middle and upper classes, and the white race."

Pat Conroy also smells sexist repression behind the magnolia mythology. These ladies' concealed ferocity, he argues, "helped them survive the impervious tyranny of Southern men more comfortable with a myth than a flesh and blood woman."

Objection sustained. The best scholarship peels away the surface to expose the truth that lurks beneath. On occasion, however, that discarded surface is just as intriguing as the truth below. If "the flower of Southern womanhood" sprang from a dark soil mulched with racism, testosterone, and guilt, does that make it wrong to admire the blossoms? For some of us the blossom, at its most splendid, is a marvel that speaks for itself. But admiration is by no means universal. In *Southern Folk, Plain and Fancy,* sociologist John Shelton Reed assembles an array of opinions pro and con. Marshall Frady once wrote—"not at all gallantly," Reed remarks—that "Southern women, on the whole, are a peculiar coy wine that does not travel well beyond its own indulgent clime. Northerners tend to find them faintly grotesque."

That's ungallant and unreliable. My guess is that Frady asked too few Yankees who had met too few ladies. According to Florence King, it's dangerous to practice ordinary courtesy on a Yankee—he'll think you're hot for him and follow you home.

If belles are a taste you don't care to acquire, humorlessness and political self-righteousness are traits that will help you to resist. No one denies that there's a certain languor, a certain comfort with idleness and privilege that attaches itself to the tradition of the Southern lady.

"Honey, I'm so exhausted," my mother-in-law once told her daughter. "I've had three men in the yard all day."

Marshall Chapman tells the story of a Spartanburg lady who suffered a flat tire on the way to a cocktail party, and solved her predicament by waving down the first trucker who came by.

"A trucker!" her friend responds, horrified. "Jenny, you could have been raped!"

"Dear, I thought of that," says the Spartanburg lady. "But I believe I can muddle my way through a rape, and the truth is I don't know a damn thing about changing a tire."

It's a crude Yankee canard that the modern belle was created by *Gone With the Wind,* which taught her mother affectations her grandmother never imagined. Anyone who honestly doubts the belle's historical antecedents should read *Recollections of a Southern Daughter,* an antebellum memoir by Cornelia Jones Pond of Liberty County, South Carolina (edited by Lucinda McKethan). Pond devotes two full pages to dressing for a party, circa 1850, as she turns herself into a human wedding cake frosted with bows and camellias.

I've been privileged to meet a few vintage belles who were grown women when Scarlett was a twinkle in Margaret Mitchell's eye. What these grand old ladies had in common with their granddaughters, and no doubt with their own grandmothers, was an overwhelming sense of social responsibility. Never mind this sultriness, which may be nothing more than Southern manners misinterpreted by aliens. Responsibility is the blessed key to a distinctly Southern, distinctly regional ladyhood. I've known Yankee ladies of measureless poise and panache. But the best of them, compared with their Southern sisters, brought more chill than thrill to my life. They had the graces and they knew the rules, but they didn't care—or they didn't care enough—if *you* fell by the wayside.

A Southern lady of gentle breeding, or even one capable of simulating it, takes responsibility for every social situation, every fragile ego within her reach. Whatever your shortcomings, she refuses to let you fail. This is her job, her calling. We know that a lady never lets a silence fall; but a Southern lady begins her vigilance where lesser social sentinels throw up their hands. If anything coarse or unfortunate (e.g., the sitcom wit of some urban Yankees) threatens the fragile social fabric she's weaving, she springs to head it off like a blue-ribbon sheepdog. If its foul foot gets in the door, she expunges the footprint with a wash bucket of Lysol-strength charm.

Watch her face, if a particularly nasty guest poses a threat to the entire evening. You'll see pure pluck and determination, a grit to match Scarlett O'Hara facing down Union foragers from the steps of Tara. If three or four true ladies are present when such a situation arises, watch the alpha belle deploy her forces and take charge. You may feel the impulse to applaud.

She'll convince you that the sun is shining on the darkest day of the year. She's the sturdy levee that protects us from the mighty river of ugliness and negativity that runs so close to all our lives. And the truest belle is the one who carries it all off with the least visible effort, the most convincing aplomb. If you hit her with a fire hose in her wedding dress, or turn a rabid dingo loose at her reception, she retains at least the shadow of her best brave smile. Courtesy and cheer will never fail her in this life.

This tradition of the Southern lady has been strong enough to adapt and survive cataclysmic social change. My wife, for example, would protest violently against any insinuation that she was ever a belle. Still, she was educated at a couple of certified Virginia belle-fries, and every summer her parents sent her to Aunt Gay-Gay in Birmingham for lady lessons that weren't available in the coal-mining country. The ladycraft she learned in Alabama has never deserted her, though she deflects any praise it attracts.

"Manners," she insists, "are just kindness. Just putting people at their ease."

My wife and many of her school friends came through the feminist revolution with a fairly happy compromise. They escaped the Junior League and embraced the new risks and possibilities—they're writers, editors, scholars, public servants, money managers—but never saddled themselves with the aggressive discipline of lockstep liberationists. They know they're supposed to be offended if someone calls them ladies. But in their hearts they're flattered.

This is no blanket endorsement of homebred Dixie darlings, nor a claim that the species is homogeneous. There are shy ladies of impeccable courtesy who eschew the glamour and decline the sober responsibility of holding society together. These conscientious objectors to bellehood make some of the best big sisters in the world. And of course there are harridans who use a fetching Delta drawl and a set of enhanced eyebrows the way Lizzie Borden used an axe.

I'm talking about the best of the breed, and I think they play a critical role in the survival of an endangered civilization—not only Southern but American civilization. In a decade when every medium proclaims that rudeness and vulgarity are the keys to the kingdom of Mammon, when Adam's lost children squander their precious lives barking into telephones and staring at electronic screens—when Niagaras of e-mail disseminate the unlanguage of the walking dead—each gracious lady of the old Southern school is a pearl beyond price. She's priestess of a lost art as important to our language, in its own way, as poetry.

In *Southern Folk*, John Reed calls another witness, Roy Reed, who puts his finger on the single greatest advantage of living among Southern Americans. Conversation in New York is "hurled stones," Roy Reed wrote in the *New York Times*. "In the South, it's moonshine passed slowly to all who care to lift the bottle."

As kinsman to Northerners who spray in my face and scare my dogs to make a point about a football coach, I'll take the moonshine, thank you ma'am.

The next time you're fortunate enough to see the moonshine coming your way, pay close attention to the woman who's passing the bottle. When the last belle has gone the way of the ivory-billed woodpecker—just an echo where the Spanish moss hangs thickest—what an impenetrable silence will fall.

God's Holy Fire

The *New York Times Book Review* has a genius for malignant mismatches between books and reviewers, a recurrent scandal that's hardening into a legend. No writer has so many admirers that the *Times* can't find one Iago to eviscerate him, no writer argues so clearly that it can't find one crank to misunderstand her. Could we expect the *Times,* as a sort of professional courtesy among higher powers, to make an exception for a book about God?

The *Book Review* has outdone itself with reviews of two serious books addressed to the Question of Questions: "Does God exist and does he care?" Reynolds Price's *Letter to a Man in the Fire*—a book in which Christ, in a vision, washes the author's wound in the Sea of Galilee—was assigned to poet Edward Hirsch. "Price's belief system seems distant and even alien to me," conceded Hirsch, a Jew. His sympathetic review was qualified by his admission that "Jesus interposes himself between this book and me."

Price, who survived a malignant tumor on his spine but lost the use of his legs, addresses this extended meditation on suffering to a young medical student dying of cancer. The book specifically tests the limits of *Christian* consolation in the Valley of the Shadow. With more than a quarter of a billion professed followers of Jesus Christ in the territorial United States and Canada, you'd think at least one—an Easter Christian, a Jansenist, a Unitarian?—might turn up in the *Book Review's* Rolodex to give Reynolds Price the fair reading he deserves.

But it was Annie Dillard's *For the Time Being,* which offers nothing less than a new theology for thinking Christians, that suffered the ultimate mismatch at the hands of the *Times*. Dillard, who gives her religious affiliation as "Catholic convert," has always worshiped in the roofless church of H. D. Thoreau and John Muir. Her life's work can be read as a passionate love/hate relationship with the created world and its elusive Creator. Her book fell into the clutches of a reviewer, Wendy Lesser, who allowed, after eight or ten paragraphs of less-than-sympathetic exegesis, "As a Jewish atheist with little or no feel for nature, I am admittedly not the ideal reader."

They couldn't find anyone who likes to take a hike, at least? Assigning a spiritually challenged, nature-blind apartment rat to review Annie Dillard is like recruiting Hermann Goering to review *The Diary of Anne Frank*. The Field Marshal might have had the grace to disqualify himself, as Wendy Lesser did not.

Such cruel pairings might be comical if most publishers and booksellers were not convinced that Sunday reviews in the *Times* are the only reviews that influence a new book's sales. But exasperation with the *Times* doesn't chill my enthusiasm for the conversation these martyred authors initiate.

There are intellectual people and spiritual people, but very few people like Price and Dillard who are both. Religion in this country has become simplistic and undemanding, a buffet of fast-food faith for a fast-buck society. Smug Christians and equally smug atheists behave as if further speculation is a waste of time. The solitary pilgrim feels that his hard-won insights are unwelcome. We brood in darkness until someone like Price or Dillard lights the candles and reassures us that it's all right to argue about God.

Why can't we talk? Even the frank disengagement of Hirsch and Lesser brings fresh air to this forum. It wasn't long ago that a Jew's opinions on Christianity, or an atheist's opinions on anything, provoked violent hostility from the Christian mainstream. ("Goys have beliefs that would shame a gorilla," says Philip Roth's Portnoy.)

As an outlaw theologian, I benefit from any dialogue. No religion worth preaching should be exempt from scrutiny or debate. In that spirit, I admit that I resist some of Price's arguments in *Letter to a*

Man in the Fire. I hope my reservations won't be dismissed because my suffering has been trivial compared with the suffering of Reynolds Price. ("The Gods who live on high have decreed that wisdom comes to man alone through suffering," sings the Chorus in Aeschylus' *Oresteia.*) Only a very coarse reader will fail to appreciate the wisdom, the pain, the honesty, and the humility to which his book bears witness. "This one long surmise," Price concludes, "comes from as deep in my mind and nature as I know how to go."

I have no patented skeptic's objection to altered states or personal visions of the divine (and neither, to his credit, did Edward Hirsch). I'm a disciple of William James, who argued in *Varieties of Religious Experience* that several millennia of private visions, reported by eloquent witnesses of every human description, constitute compelling evidence that there's far more here under heaven than most of us can see or explain.

Can I myself claim an epiphany, a personal glimpse of the divine? If you put the bar high enough—a voice, a miraculous intervention, a daylight sighting of a celestial celebrity—the answer is, no, none. If you place the bar a little lower—a momentary parting of the veil, what Wordsworth called an "intimation of immortality"—the answer is, sure, thousands. The bad news for Wendy Lesser is that these Close Encounters are more common out in "nature" than, say, in Bloomingdale's.

I'm all for visions, and envious of visionaries. It's Job, not Jesus, who "interposes himself between this book and me." Price, for obvious reasons, has chosen the Book of Job as his paradigm for the one-sided covenant between God and men. Though it's most admirable as literature, the Book of Job portrays God in a manner I always found hateful and perverse. Read it again and you'll see that it's the best example, in an Old Testament packed with examples, of what I call the "fascist" theological fallacy.

In prehistoric times heaven and earth stood sixty feet apart—whirlwinds spoke to us and bushes burned without consuming themselves. Each lightning bolt was an angry god hunting sinners, and every clap of thunder was the bass voice of his rage. The Hebrews, no less than any ancient people, conceived of the highest power in terms of force and fear.

Some of us, over the past few millennia, have managed to outgrow the Big Massa model. God may crush me utterly, grind me into molecules, expunge my name from the rolls—who am I, anyway?—but he can't make me admire him for it. Or worship or honor him. If he seems less scrupulous, less guided by conscience than I am, what is he but one colossal bully? The god of Job is a gangster god, a vain, cruel, irresponsible despot, unworthy of a good man like Job.

I'm sure the story was intended as a parable, an illustration of one man's helplessness in the grip of his fate. It was probably written by someone far more subtle than most Christians and Jews who accept it as holy writ and fair warning. Like so many biblical stories, the Book of Job was adapted from an earlier model, the Babylonian poem "I Will Praise the Lord of Wisdom" (seventh century B.C.), in which a righteous nobleman is tormented and finally rehabilitated by the capricious god Marduk.

I stand with Ivan Karamazov—Price unjustly chides him as "sophomoric"—when he swears that he cannot bow to a god who tortures a single innocent child. But I can't imagine a god who tortures, or permits torture he's able to prevent, any more than I can imagine a god who's gratified by our cringing submission. If God is unable to recognize "bad" in human terms—if he has no problem with Auschwitz or the tidal wave that drowned 138,000 Bangladeshi—how can we believe that he sees "good" in human terms, as in justice, mercy, and brotherly love?

But that's logic, mere human reason deployed disrespectfully against the Faith of Our Fathers. Martin Luther was especially clear on the status of reason among Christians: "Reason is the devil's bride," Luther rails, "a beautiful whore, and God's worst enemy. Whoever wants to be a Christian should tear the eyes out of his reason. Tread her underfoot. Throw dung in her face. You must part with reason and kill her, or you will not get into the kingdom of heaven."

If thy brain offends thee, pluck it out. "Christianity demands the crucifixion of the intellect," adds Kierkegaard.

Hogwash. With all due respect, Luther's outburst—a protesteth-too-much that probably betrays a cankerous doubt—is desperate and blasphemous. To refuse to use your head is as sacrilegious as refusing to use your eyes or your hands. In Christian terms, we insult the Creator by refusing his gifts. And reason, with all its limitations, is the great gift that separates human beings from the beasts of the field.

If reason whispers that a loving, caring god cannot be reconciled with an all-seeing, all-powerful god, why not listen to reason? This is where Reynolds Price appears to stumble, at what Annie Dillard calls "the old fatal-to-reason belief, that we suffer at the hands of God omnipotent."

It's a conundrum that spawned some of the most tortured thinking and indigestible theology in the annals of organized religion. Personally I'd rather be the victim of blind forces, oblivious to my existence, than the passive pawn of some Master of the Universe who delights in fooling me and thwarting me at every turn. The most "human" God I ever imagined was a kind of Sorcerer's Apprentice, who started it all and quickly, haplessly lost control. God never seemed enigmatic or "inscrutable" to me because I never cast him in my image or expected him to behave in any manner I could hope to interpret. Or to "behave" at all.

"God doesn't do things, God *is* things," I read somewhere recently. I can't express my own belief more eloquently than that. Annie Dillard can, and where she can't she knows of a sage who will speak in her place. It's fair to say that no one writes or thinks quite like Dillard. Within one skin you get a god-haunted poet/pilgrim and a deadpan comic who punctuates a passage of the most sublime (or horrific) speculation with a wisecrack. Who else but Annie Dillard would write, "I don't know beans about God"?

As an essayist Dillard works in collage, patching and layering with things that seem scarcely related to each other, teasing the reader, without any sense of urgency, toward some very ambitious ideas. A formidable researcher, she's a one-woman archive of the arcane facts and neglected wisdom of the ages. A lover of numbers, she's a collector of dreadful ones: 750,000 Chinese killed in the Tangshan earthquake of 1976, an annual death toll of thirty million children under age five, two thousand suicides every day.

Along with such horrors as birth defects ("What about the bird-headed dwarf?") and the flaying alive (with horses' currycombs) of the eighty-five-year-old Rabbi Akiva in 135 A.D., Dillard marshals her awful numbers for what some will take as a bill of indictment—for negligence and callousness, if not for murder—of Almighty God himself. Yet her verdict is "Not guilty, by virtue of mistaken identity." The dangerously butch Old Testament God who might have been implicated in these crimes never existed, except in the minds of ancestors long dead and buried.

Will the real God please stand up? Reynolds Price, like Dillard, presents a list of grievances, personal and universal, that weigh against our belief in a just and merciful (and all-powerful) God. "Our hardest challenge," he writes, "becomes an effort to imagine how such a God can be truly and usefully said to love us." Hard indeed. But Price rises to the challenge, conceding only that he now rejects "Father" as a useful way of imagining his God. ("What definition of *father* even begins to hint at the deepest dark in the nature of what is called—most perilously—God the Father?")

Price emerges from this inquiry as Job emerged from his ordeals—burned but not apostate, not despairing. A stoic at peace with his belief that "God loves his creation, whatever his kind of *love* means for you and me."

I'm dumb with admiration, yet not persuaded. If Price's optimism is ingrained and incurable, as he claims, my stubborn Unitarian rationalism is no less so. At the risk of evoking a famous sinner, I'd answer "Does God exist and does he care?" with "Define 'God'—define 'exist'—define 'care.'"

The Book of Job is a rock that breaks all but the toughest Christians. Dillard's modest proposals—there's no hectoring or proselytizing in either of these books—offer the rest of us a way to steer around it. Acquit God of all charges; strip him of the terror and testosterone of the Old Testament and the improbable tenderness of the New. Relieve poor God of the thankless task of loving, judging, rewarding, and punishing the incorrigible race of men. Remove God from the center of the human dilemma and build him up along its edges, with holy things we can feel and sense for ourselves.

"'God,'" Dillard writes, "is the awareness of the infinite in each of us."

"Pan-entheism" is her word for it, and she quotes a theologian who calls it "the private view" of most Christian intellectuals today. It's the opposite of atheism because its successful practice requires constant spiritual vigilance—an eye peeled, an ear to the ground to detect the divine. She finds its essence in a pair of lovely quotations.

The Jesuit Teilhard de Chardin: "By means of all created things, without exception, the divine assails us, penetrates us, and molds us. We imagined it as distant and inaccessible, whereas in fact we live steeped in its burning layers."

And an interpreter of the eighteenth-century Hasidic holy man, the Baal Shem Tov: "When you walk across the field with your mind pure and holy, then from all the stones, and from all growing things, and all animals, the sparks of their souls come out and cling to you, and then they are purified and become a holy fire in you."

To the pilgrim in me, those words are worth ten thousand sermons and a dozen cathedrals. God and reason can coexist; thinking and believing can be reconciled. Universalists and transcendentalists were telling us that all along. And in pan-entheism an honored place remains for Grace, the last theological comfort most Christians would be willing to relinquish. What is Grace—an unearned, supernatural sense that hope is not in vain—but each individual's reassurance that he, too, is standing in the holy fire?

These speculations won't set off a second Reformation, not in a society where three-quarters of us claim to believe in angels, and fundamentalist broadcasters prosper with doctrine that insults our intelligence as recklessly as professional wrestling. But they're a place to start, and a beacon in the fog for the disillusioned minority that might become drab atheists because they think there's nowhere else to go.

IV

SWEET HOME CAROLINA

But Now I See

But Now I See

I have seen the David, seen the Mona Lisa too
And I have heard Doc Watson play Columbus Stockade Blues.
—Guy Clark, *Dublin Blues*

The Merle Watson Festival is a four-day celebration that stops only to sleep, and not for long either. By day four, a Sunday, even younger people try to pace themselves. But one promising Sunday morning four or five years ago, we committed ourselves to a sunrise gospel session, which meant coffee in the dark and a long drive down the mountain in the fog. Our commitment was rewarded, beyond all mortal expectations, by a once-in-a-lifetime gospel trio of Doc Watson, Ralph Stanley, and Emmylou Harris.

We came in on "Heaven's Bright Shore," followed by "Rank Stranger" and "I'll Pass Over Thee." For an hour or so, forty lucky pilgrims shared a privileged preview of Hillbilly Heaven. I feel sorry for ticketholders who actually went to church that Sunday morning. I'm afraid they were cheated, because there in the corner of the gospel tent—singing along in a soft clear bass—was a big old mountaineer with a salt-and-pepper ponytail who looked an awful lot like God.

The trio wound up their set with "Amazing Grace." Harris wore her church face and sang the high notes like a bourbon-frosted angel. Stanley stood ramrod straight like he does, like he's standing to hear his sentence in the court of Final Judgment. When they reached "I once was blind, but now I see," I took a hard look at Doc Watson to see if I could pick up anything wistful or ironic on his face.

Doc just looked comfortable and spiritual, the same as he looked when he played at my college in 1963, in the heat of the great folk revival. New England had never seen anything like Doc. For weeks after, preppies from Connecticut with expensive Martin guitars were trying to lower their voices and flat-pick their own way through "Tennessee Stud." A year earlier, half of them had been listening to Fabian.

I was stunned by Doc's performance, and suspected for the first time that those mountains, which I'd been trying to escape all my life, might be harboring things I ought to be proud of. In those days it was still possible, I think, for an unsophisticated person to be ambushed by sheer authenticity, to be knocked flat and left in the road by something undeniably real.

I never imagined that he'd be my neighbor someday, that I'd buy a house just two ridges over from the Watson homeplace and get to hear Doc play for free at his cousin's twelve-table fish restaurant on the road to Boone, North Carolina, under a sign that says "Friends Gather Here."

I suppose I've seen him perform a hundred times. Most worthwhile people know that Doc Watson is a blind guitarist, blind not quite from birth but from infancy. Over the years Doc's almost convinced me that blindness is no obstacle for a born musician.

"Music is sound," Watson told one interviewer. "You learn where the notes are because of the sound of them. You don't have to see to play the guitar."

From watching Doc, I'll even argue that there's a different quality to a blind musician's performance, often a superior quality. When he makes the connection with his audience, it's all-consuming. He's so much with them because it's his one moment, his chance—because when the connection is broken he's so much alone.

Backstage, Doc sits immobile, supernaturally patient, with what I interpret as exquisitely tuned attention. I believe he could hear a string break or a note misplayed three tents away, over the roar of the multitude. The ears of blind musicians are the finest instruments they own. Ray Charles recently heard the Rolling Stones live and declared their decibel level unbearable. "I thought I'd gone deaf," said Charles, "and God, I'm already blind."

My wife had a great uncle, Blind Bill Smith of Buchanan County, Virginia, who was a locally famous piano player. Like Doc Watson, Blind Bill sometimes tuned pianos for a living. He was notoriously hard-living, for a man with such a disability, until he found Jesus late in life. It was an experience he related to his brother in a series of letters I'm still reading.

"It is true that I have missed the beauties of this world," Blind Bill wrote home, "but it is great to know that I will see in a world that is more beautiful than this one."

Blind Bill's letters made me reconsider Doc Watson. Does Doc feel that he's missed the beauties of this world? To me Doc Watson *is* one of the beauties of this world. I'd never mention his handicap— Doc prefers to call it "a hindrance"—if I didn't feel a trace of guilt. A great blind musician may be one of the few members of the human race who gives a lot more to the world than he ever gets back.

We're a selfish audience. We're the ones who benefit because Doc Watson had so much time to practice, so few distractions and temptations compared with Hank Williams or George Jones.

Watson, who just turned seventy-six, was born the same year as Hank Williams—Doc was six months older. Country music has a history of cautionary tales, of stars who killed or lobotomized themselves with whiskey and drugs, or peaked early and spent their last forty years impersonating themselves on the Grand Ole Opry, singing the same three songs. So many of the great ones left us wishing they could have left us more. As much as he hated the life on the road ("the loneliness . . . but I had a family to feed"), Doc paid his dues and minded his music, and now he's outlasting them all.

We got our money's worth out of Doc Watson. Does Doc think it's been a fair exchange, all things considered? I never asked him. I'm shy around people I admire, and musical geniuses make me, a non-musician, feel like a tourist. I only introduced myself, and shook Doc's hand, on one occasion. He was in Greensboro to receive one of his many folk arts awards, and I found him sitting alone in a class-room behind the stage area, waiting for an escort.

I don't think he heard me come in. It was an unfair advantage to take, but I watched him for five minutes before I spoke. It wasn't much of a conversation—two polite strangers, each caught out of his element in a different way.

If you want to hear Doc wax effusive, I've been told, start by prais-ing Merle. Doc Watson's long, much-honored late career is an In-dian summer any artist would envy, but it followed a hard, hard frost. The defining tragedy of Doc's life was the death in 1985 of his only son, Merle, a superb slide-guitar player who rolled a tractor over on himself one night up in Watauga County.

It was Doc's relentless grief that generated the Merle Watson Fes-tival, which has convened in Wilkesboro, North Carolina, every April since 1988. Though it's grown tremendously in size and renown—crowds reach fifty thousand now—Doc has never let his huge picnic lose its focus as a memorial to his son. In four days at Wilkesboro, you'll hear the name Merle a thousand times.

Merlefest, as they call it, is unique. It's not a fiddler's convention or a folk festival. It's more of a family reunion, a gathering of the clans where the names of the dear departed—not only Merle Watson but Bill Monroe and Carter Stanley and Mother Maybelle—are heard far more often than any names from the charts.

Merlefest is about remembering, about respect for your elders. It's inspiring to watch kids like Iris Dement and Alison Krauss sing with Doc for the first time ever. Or to hear Guy Clark—looking none too well-preserved himself—sing the songs he's written in honor of Doc Watson and Ramblin' Jack Elliott, legends of a previous generation who are sitting in back of him, grinning.

Up on his mountain, Doc is still the man. Every April the country aristocracy, the best musicians from Nashville and the bluegrass cir-cuit, come to the mountain to say, "We love you, Doc." And God knows to hear him perform. A musician can tell you whether Doc Watson is still unchallenged king of the flat-pickers. The miracle, to me, is that Doc is singing better now than he was twenty years ago. Whatever it took to temper and refine that warm honey baritone— age, grief, singing in the dark—the big voice we're hearing now is often the best one on the program. "A voice pure as mountain water," a critic wrote last year.

Flatlanders come up to Wilkesboro to buy nostalgia—"Is he still performing?"—and go away raving about Doc's voice and the incredible range of his repertoire. Doc loves to rock, they're surprised to learn. He spent the '50s playing electric guitar in a dance band, and rockabilly suits him fine, especially Carl Perkins's "Blue Suede Shoes."

He's never sounded better. He has more friends than The Library, and folklorists call him "a national treasure," which is no exaggeration. People might think that Doc Watson has everything he could reasonably ask for, at this stage of his life. But we can't ever know how another man feels about his luck, any more than we can know how he feels playing for ten thousand people he can't see. Maybe these festivals we love just remind him of how much it hurt to lose his boy.

These are only a fan's notes—but I despise the word "fan." It's a low-country, Disneyland kind of word, spawned by mass entertainment. They don't talk about fans in Deep Gap. Dock Boggs and Tommy Jarrell, Clarence Ashley, they had friends, neighbors, and appreciative audiences. They didn't have "fans." Hank Williams had fans, and Elvis Presley—and look what happened to them.

Just call this a personal appreciation. I never cared about celebrities; I'm fascinated by people who do something difficult incredibly well. I've become attached to just a few, and I've praised too many of them after they were dead. Doc, alive and kicking over in Deep Gap, is probably feeling better than I do, maybe humming "Wildwood Flower" and tuning his guitar as we speak. If someone should read this to him, I hope he understands that it isn't a story some reporter was assigned to write. It's a personal appreciation by an admirer who's invading Doc's privacy the only way he dares, and saying thank you the only way he knows how.

On the Road Again

Wherever I travel, I'm an energetic one-man Chamber of Commerce for the state of North Carolina. When a foreigner or Yankee asks me why I live there, I remind him that North Carolina is more generously endowed with mountains and seashore than any state east of California. I mention our barbecue cooks, who are guilty of the nation's most creative and irresistible abuses against the rights of pigs. I mention the prairies of tobacco and the endless forests of pines and condominiums that spring from our red soil.

If they demand unique, I point to Biltmore House and the burial place of Chang and Eng, the original Siamese Twins. Or Raleigh's Museum of Political Antiquities and Curiosities (insiders know it as the Congressional Club), where we maintain living specimens of political animals that have been extinct in most areas of North America for fifty years.

Then someone asks me to explain lying-in-the-road deaths. That's right—lying in the road. According to records kept by Dr. Lawrence Harris, who teaches pathology at East Carolina University, North Carolina not only leads the nation in these peculiar fatalities, but leads by such a wide margin that we allow our closest competitor no hope of challenging for the prize. In one four-year period, Dr. Harris documented 136 authentic lying-in-the-road deaths in North Carolina. We averaged better than one death every two weeks. Since the distant runners-up have borders with North Carolina—Georgia peels them up at less than 40 percent of our pace, Tennessee at a little better than 20 percent—there's no question that we live at the lying-in-the-road center of America. The Southwest is littered with the pressed carcasses of armadillos. Up here we decorate the asphalt with possums and people. Human road meat is a Tar Heel specialty.

Dr. Harris's study made a big splash when it was published in the *New York Times*. New Yorkers can understand how an occasional wino will get pressed flat by a sanitation truck, in the big city where there are so many winos and so little space for them all to stretch out. But it's hard for them to imagine a vast landscape where there are so many people lying in the road that motorists are unable to avoid them. If there are dozens of drunks stretched out in the road, how many more are lying in the cornfield or staggering along the creek? It gives them a distorted impression of our drinking.

In a morbidly droll editorial headed "Liquored Up, Smashed Flat," the *Wilmington Star-News* addressed the questions, "Why us, why here?" Since there doesn't appear to be an actual army of drunks stumbling across our farmland and perishing in our rivers, how does such a large percentage of the available talent find its way to the yellow line and to eternity?

Dr. Harris, who came to North Carolina in 1978, reported only two cases of lying-in-the-road death in his ten years as a pathologist in Vermont. In his effort to determine the particularly Southern and rural character of the phenomenon, and to explain how North Carolina comes to be the special preserve of these tragic human possums, he maintained strict criteria for his statistics. His study excluded all road deaths with any hint of suicide, and all deaths where the victim was thrown from a vehicle and subsequently run over. In the pure cases that he retained, there were several consistent elements. Most of the deaths occurred after dark in the summer, in rural areas on two-lane country roads. Autopsies showed that most of the victims were outrageously drunk, many of them comatose. Ninety percent of them were men. A significant number had been convicted of driving under the influence and had their driver's licenses revoked.

This sorry fraternity of road warriors was perfectly integrated—sixty-eight blacks, sixty-eight whites. From the circumstantial evidence that he accumulated, the doctor fashioned a theory. The key, he believes, is the summer heat. Our annual heat wave, with the inert air mass just cooking on the land and cooking everything in it, with the roads too hot for bare feet or thin shoes in the daytime—this is the season for lying in the road.

According to Dr. Harris, the drunk is lurching along the road at the ragged edge of consciousness, free of all rational process that could accurately be described as human. Perhaps his last recognizable thought was that he was never going to make it to his bed, or that the woman at home was never going to let him share it in this condition. The concentration of alcohol in his blood will cause his body to lose heat rapidly, in spite of the temperature. What's left of his brain will record on some primitive level that the only heat he can feel is coming up through his shoes from the road. The road invites him to lie down and feel the heat all along his body. Once prone he's unconscious.

Lying in the road for warmth—exactly like the possum, which produces such a spectacular harvest of road meat in North Carolina. The lowly possum, which sits almost at the bottom of the order of mammals when it comes to intelligence. If you ever doubted alcohol's capacity to throw evolution into reverse, consider the strange phenomenon of lying in the road.

Dr. Harris was less successful when he tried to explain why North Carolina's country roads, in particular, encourage so many of its citizens to lie down and die. At this stage of his research, the best he could offer was, "I think it has a lot to do with warm weather, alcohol abuse, and poverty." We seem to have more than our share of all three. The study reminded me of William Friday's comment when he chaired a survey of poverty in North Carolina: "What we really have here are two distinct societies." On the high side of one society, they're Dancing in the Dark; on the down side of the other society, they're Lying in the Road. A police officer explained to me why the Breathalyzer sometimes gets almost impossible readings on motorists arrested for DWI, readings indicating that the subject could scarcely breathe, far less drive. They're motorists who've artificially extended their consciousness with cocaine. The possum class, the class that dies in the road, can't afford the cocaine to keep them awake.

The authorities were impressed with Dr. Harris and his research, but dismayed because no remedy is apparent. If road crews scattered nails and broken glass on the pavement to discourage overnight guests, it would play hell with our tires. In driver education classes they frighten drinking drivers with films of horrible crashes and mutilations, but what would lure the alcoholic pedestrian to see horror films of human pancakes? Dr. Harris isn't optimistic.

"In the end," he says, "the most sardonic and cynical thing you can say is that we've defined here a baseline of human behavior which no traffic safety measure will ever be able to correct." The only word of caution that might be effective would be a word to teenage drivers, who like to exercise their high gears on the back roads, where they know they're unlikely to encounter radar. That thing in the passing lane might not be a tenderized possum or a roll of insulation. It might be Uncle Dan.

Unsafe at Any Speed

The gracious Old South of shantytowns and shuttered factories, chain gangs and carnivorous sheriffs in Ray-Bans. Hollywood, with a script by Erskine Caldwell, turned a selective reality of the '30s into its myth of a dark and alien land where violence, like collard greens, was always bubbling on someone's back burner. Tourists were repelled, Northern liberals petrified, investment capital hard to come by.

Progressive Southerners, who battled these stereotypes for generations, had reason to believe they were making headway. Then came the elections of November 1994, packing Southern legislatures with late-model reactionaries who do not dishonor the memory of Bull Connor or Lester Maddox.

If you loved *Cool Hand Luke, Easy Rider, The Defiant Ones, Mississippi Burning,* and *In the Heat of the Night*—and pulled for the bad guys—the second-millennium South may pluck at your heartstrings like a Stephen Foster medley. Even those colorful chain gangs are back, in Alabama and in Florida, where a get-tough state senator named "Chain Gang Charlie" Crist succeeded in reversing fifty years of bleeding-heart penal reforms. Out in the Everglades shackled inmates are chopping away at jungle vegetation with machetes, dawn to dusk. As a result of Chain Gang Charlie's no-coddling crusade, they get no sunscreen and no bug repellent to ward off the swarming swamp mosquitoes—just thick leather pants and gardening gloves to give them a sporting chance against the water moccasins.

That's hard time, Jack. And there's harder coming. We have governors who run for reelection on the death sentences they refused to commute, and sheriffs who campaign on their reputations for making prisoners miserable.

In Davidson County, North Carolina, a throwback Republican sheriff named Gerald Hege rules a 560-square-mile police state where crime fighters are more frightening than criminals. Hege was a railroad signal repairman whose career in law enforcement had ended twenty years ago, when a previous sheriff fired him for beating a prisoner (he'd also shot one suspect to death). Resurrected in the infamous election of 1994, Sheriff Hege dresses like an Army commando, carries a five-foot hickory shillelagh like his idol Buford "Walking Tall" Pusser, and wears an unconcealed pistol in church. He has a spider web painted on his patrol car. In his jail there's no TV, no mattresses between 6 A.M. and 11 P.M., no reading material except the Bible. Prisoners go to work in the striped pajamas of the 1950s.

Hege's reign of terror has tripled fights and "incidents" in the Davidson County jail and coincides with a 10 percent increase in crime countywide. Other law-enforcement agencies deplore and avoid him. But for many of his rural constituents he's the law-and-order folk hero of their TV-tempered dreams. Stocks and thumbscrews, whipping posts, even selected lynchings make sense to the voter who admires Sheriff Hege.

An abiding curse of the Southland is that our native fools are so picturesque. But the war on "criminals"—not quite the same as the war on crime—isn't limited to the stubborn South. Eighty-two Americans were executed in the first ten months of 1999. With more than three thousand customers on Death Row, the body count this year could easily top one hundred. In Utah, thousands of citizens volunteered for the firing squad that executed child-killer John Albert Taylor.

The notorious Los Angeles Police Department has settled ninety-one claims of police brutality for record $7.5 million; the city of Philadelphia has paid out over $2 million. Nearly every new crime bill, in Congress or in the legislatures, aims to make it harder for defendants to defend themselves and harder for convicts, especially condemned ones, to appeal. America's prison population, swollen by mandatory sentencing laws, has tripled since 1980 and stands at a record high of nearly 1.2 million inmates. Our incarceration rate is four times China's, ten times Ireland's, half again as high as South Africa's.

This is the land of the lockup. No other nation on earth comes close. And most statistics show that violent crime is declining, especially in the big cities. Naturally the Right claims that tough guys like Mark Fuhrman and Sheriff Hege are getting the job done, and even that criminals are hesitating now that concealed handguns are everywhere.

Criminologists, on the other hand, credit "community policing"— patrolmen on foot who become a familiar presence in the high-crime neighborhoods they formerly cruised in squad cars with tinted windshields. Only front-end, before-the-fact strategies like community policing ever made any sense to me. For years I've harbored a suspicion that deterrence is sheer fantasy, based on a false analogy between the aberrant or "criminal" mind and more conventional models. Neither the electric chair, the snake-infested swamp, the five-foot hickory club, the tiny stifling cell without TV, or even the mortification of wearing stripes in public was *ever once* considered at the moment a violent crime was perpetrated. The criminal was either doing "magical thinking"—imagining that he alone was exempt from consequences and the laws of cause and effect—or he wasn't thinking at all.

Throw out deterrence, of course, and hard-line rhetoric collapses, leaving us with institutionalized revenge. Pressed with research they can't refute, proponents of capital punishment and hard time will wave away all the facts—in rare candid moments—and admit that revenge is the thing.

Does that mean liberals, who are losing the elections and the initiative, are at least winning the debate? Not at all. Liberals who stress rehabilitation, therapy, and empathy for the abused and disadvantaged criminal are exhausting their credibility in the world's most violent nation. Can't we make good citizens of murderers and sex offenders, if we just find the key to their pain? Career criminals find these liberals amusing, and very useful. By and large, an individual who can't be deterred can't be rehabilitated, either. If the stick fails, so does the carrot.

No one seems to get it right. Criminal justice is the great American exception. Consider the first thing every investigative reporter learns at his editor's knee: "Follow the money." Wherever there's a totally irrational status quo—health care, campaign funding, even handgun worship—it's probably that way because someone makes a lot of money maintaining it.

You know you've stumbled into a region of unreason, bordering on pathology, when you look at the bottom line on crime. Each citizen in prison costs the taxpayer ten times what he costs on parole or probation; each prisoner executed represents an unconscionable sum, the net worth of at least one wealthy American. Thanks to the Christian Right and other self-elected guardians of other people's morals, we waste billions fighting illegal drug sales, gambling, prostitution, and other victimless crimes. No one has calculated the cost of trials that attempt to prove the legal sanity (for purposes of legal revenge) of drooling psychos who need strong medication to sit still in the courtroom.

All of this in a climate of tax cuts, budget slashing, and taxpayer rebellions. We suffer from a sick obsession with our criminals; the conundrum of crime and punishment is that compassion and vindictiveness are equally irrelevant. They're emotional traps—two sides of an archaic paternalism that stood for justice back when we all belonged to tribes and families. Legal codes attempted to replace the vendettas and religious taboos of primitive societies but ended up perpetuating their spirit. Our law sounds dry on the page but it's all about sin and expiation, repentance, atonement, redemption. It's about humanity wrestling, through the wretched surrogates in our prisons, with the dark inside us all.

These religious themes are heavy baggage. None of them signify in a disintegrating, secular megasociety dedicated—some would say prostituted—to the freedom of the individual. Crime isn't a theological problem. It's a social problem, a problem of public safety and public health.

The real test of our principles is the sex criminal. Conservatives recommend ropes and pitchforks. Liberals stubbornly counsel him, parole him, jail him and parole him again. But there's compelling evidence that chronic sex offenders are immune to rehabilitation. Take North Carolina's Rickey Lee Bright, a child-rape specialist. He put in sixteen years as a model prisoner, finally won a contested parole, and immediately raped another child and disappeared. I have a thick folder documenting similar cases, most of them involving deviates who escalated to more horrible crimes each time they were paroled.

Sex offenders seem to be the most patient predators on earth, and the most immutable. I don't understand why people shoot a lion that mauls a child at the zoo, but assign social workers to a human-shaped thing that rapes babies and cuts off their arms. This is not a criminal so much as a defective specimen, a flawed organism. Its "rights" don't seem relevant to me.

"Victims' rights" movements focus on revenge, which is always disappointing. It's the rights of the next victim that ought to concern us. In a rational state, fighting crime means separating the innocent, who honor the social contract, from the warped, impaired, and ferocious who will not or cannot. Even punishment is a concept that misleads us. Quarantine is the thing.

Sanity, impossible to quantify, need not be a bone of contention. For rapists, chronic sex offenders, and most classes of murderers, public safety probably requires a new category: Unsafe at any speed.

What many of these predators actually deserve is worse than anything we have the stomach to do to them. But we, the sane, prove we're sane by treating even subhumans humanely. Logic dictates a new kind of penal colony for criminals we judge to be hopelessly flawed. Conditions wouldn't have to be harsh, but quarantine would be permanent (a final test to see if deterrence exists). These colonies would concentrate our financial resources where the need is greatest. They'd provide an invaluable laboratory for criminologists and psychologists—and maybe an appropriate job for Sheriff Gerald Hege.

Father, Forgive Me

Novelist and columnist G. D. Gearino wrote a graceful tribute to his father, and admiring it I realized I'd never written anything about mine. Maybe every father with a son in the writing trade deserves at least one of these family portraits, especially if the father's no longer living and the son has something nice to say. What occasion would be more fitting than the close conjunction of Memorial Day, Father's Day, and the anniversary of my father's death? And of course I'd been grilling out, and grilling out never fails to make me think of my father.

I was working on the expensive gas grill my wife gave me for Christmas, a formidable machine that produces, in a matter of seconds, enough heat to barbecue a small heretic with some baked potatoes on the side. How this high-tech monster would have amazed and probably disgusted my father. He worked for years with a wretched little grease-caked hibachi like you see at every garage sale, and never graduated beyond a $25 charcoal grill—he never owned one with a cover, which he would have regarded as effete.

The alarming thing about my father as a grill chef was his impatience with slow briquets and his willingness to goose them with anything flammable. I saw him use gasoline, kerosene, transmission fluid, and sludge from someone's oil change he found in his shed—every petroleum product the instructions on the bag of charcoal tell you never, never to try. We ate beef seared with everything but napalm. Sometimes I'd find a little pellet of poisonous-tasting carbon stuck to the underside of my T-bone.

There were tremendous bursts of flame when he tossed in his

match, or sometimes a lighted cigarette. One Sunday he smeared the charcoal with an unidentifiable mess from a rusted can, and the blast singed his eyebrows and chest hair. The trick was to toss the match and spring away back-pedaling; in his fifties he was still surprisingly quick.

When he fired up I'd cower by a lilac bush twenty feet from the flash zone, counseling caution. He was not a man of action or a man who courted risks, my father. But he had a great misplaced confidence that nothing in the physical world could defeat him, at least nothing so humble as a charcoal grill or an outboard motor. Of course he never cooked or prepared anything indoors. Men of his generation got away with the self-serving myth that the kitchen contained mysteries beyond their grasp. My father could operate a thirty-foot fishing boat but not an electric can opener, and he found it impossible to manufacture a sandwich.

Something of a dandy for an academic, he usually wore a coat and tie, often a vest as well. But when he grilled, in the privacy of his backyard behind a fifteen-foot hedge of wild roses, my father went topless over a pair of Navy-issue khaki shorts that hung below his knees, NBA style. On hot summer days he'd sweat them through till there was no dry patch visible—fierce perspiration was another genetic legacy I'd have passed up if I'd been given the choice.

He taught me to enjoy steaks the way he prepared them, bloody inside a rich crust of carcinogenic carbon. He loved to bait "the peasants," usually members of my mother's family, who took their meat well-done. As a child I was an awed spectator at the grilling ritual. But when I reached my late teens he began to share his martinis with me and put me to work as a sous-chef, usually wielding a hose or a watering can to keep the flames from consuming the meat and half the shrubbery.

Those were the best of times for me, the best I can remember with my father when he was still in his prime and I was old enough to amuse him. For me a dry martini was always the shortest distance between a malignant universe and a benign one. Martinis made my father expansive and approachable, which he was not as a rule. He laughed in two frequencies, a rib-rattling bass rumble and an incongruous high-pitched giggle. Sometimes when he drank he'd speak in tongues, dazzling me with words and phrases from a dozen languages he couldn't actually speak. He collected them because he loved the way they sounded. We talked about sports, religion, women, and politics. And more seriously about money, work, and ambition, of which both of us have been charged with an insufficiency.

Picture a tall, underdeveloped-looking white boy with a Ricky Nelson brush cut, a nearsighted boy wearing thick glasses with geeky black plastic frames à la Buddy Holly, only geeks weren't cool in 1962 and I'd never heard of Buddy Holly. Picture a small, trim bald man in his forties, known for his good looks when he had hair, a man somehow dapper even half-naked in droopy, soaked Navy shorts; a man from the prewar generation for whom a cocktail in one hand and a cigarette in the other were accessories as natural as a fedora and two-tone shoes. I don't know who ever saw us out there drinking—my mother and brother rarely ventured out—unless it was the Kaufman kids from next door, peering through the hedge in bewilderment to see if Dad's towering inferno was a threat to burn their home.

Father and son. Senior and junior. There's something especially intimidating about carrying the same name as your father, a burden that Roy Blount, Jr., explores at chapter length in his memoir *Be Sweet*. A son so closely identified with his father tends to get a mixed message: He can't fail at life so miserably that he embarrasses the old man, but he shouldn't make such a success that he eclipses him, either.

Even if my name had been Hector, my father would have been a tough act to follow. Disapproving women say of such men, "He's in love with the sound of his own voice." And a rare voice it was, a full pulpit baritone with a fine singing range and room-shaking volume when he chose to turn it loose. I was never so mortified as when he sang his favorite hymns so loud that the Methodists turned around in their pews to stare. On the other hand, I was never so impressed as when he stood silent during the Apostles' Creed, so conspicuously silent with his big voice—silent because he was raised a Universalist and wouldn't recite anything he didn't believe.

When I first understood what he was doing with his silence—legitimizing nonconformity, rejecting peer pressure, making a public show of dissenting principle—it probably influenced me as profoundly as anything he ever offered me. My father had no time for public opinion or group-think of any kind, and on this score I'm sure I've never disappointed him.

Of course there's a downside to a father like mine. Here was a great big voice that issued judgments, swift and stern, from a swirling cloud of smoke. In my Bible School days I must have confused him with the God of Moses. Whatever doubts he may have had about himself or anything else, he did not wear them on his sleeve. An over-confident father rarely raises confident sons. On the few occasions when I take myself into the shop for a psychological tune-up—just light maintenance really, anger management, attitude adjustment—the counselor always diagnoses me with a violent aversion to authority, and my father is always the scapegoat.

When you open this door, as Gearino and Blount must have discovered, the stories and associations just tumble out and start racing in all directions. There's no closure, as the psychobabblers call it, when the subject is Dad. No matter how long he's been gone. A friend of mine in his seventies told me that it was hard to focus on his relationship with his son—age fifty—because he'd never resolved his relationship with his father, who'd been dead for thirty years.

In Ethan Canin's story "The Year of Getting to Know Us," a father tells his son, "You don't have to worry about getting to know me, because one day you're going to grow up and then you are going to *be* me."

This is the last laugh all fathers, beloved or belittled, will have on all sons. There are time bombs lurking in our chromosomes, genetic traps that were set before we were born. Sometimes it's scary. We resist by parading small victories that prove we're not clones. Of all the milder forms of human stupidity, I suppose I hate cigarettes the most.

I've never smoked one. I hate them because my father's smoke screen kept us even further apart—I'm allergic to the stuff—and because they killed him and I miss him. But in a hundred other ways he's creeping up on me, and there's no way to distinguish what he taught me from what he buried in my blood.

Once he was the dude with a hundred suits and I was the hippy with one ratty blazer who mocked him. Now my closets are filling up, mysteriously, with clothes I don't need. When I'm not working I read all day, every day, just as he did back when I was trying desperately to get his attention. I'm starting to pull away from people a little, the way he did in his fifties. Even some of his famous eccentricities—like his rule that no one but blood kin was welcome in our house after sundown—are beginning to make sense to me now.

I still like to drink martinis, though not as often or as many as we used to. And when the sun gets low over the crape myrtles I still go out to the back fence, as often as I can, and start my fire. The backyard grill is the one middle-class, wholesome, suburban all-American habit I've kept up all my life, even when my hair was so long I had to tie it back to keep it out of the coals. I'd hesitate to say this about anything else, even now, but I'm better at it than my father was. And I never use diesel fuel.

The Cedars of Lebanon

Annihilating all that's made
To a green thought in a green shade.
— Andrew Marvell, "The Garden"

The city fathers of Oxford, Mississippi, voted to celebrate William Faulkner's one hundredth birthday by commissioning a monument to Oxford's most famous native son. To clear a place in the courthouse square the novelist immortalized, they set their chainsaws to an old magnolia tree.

Faulkner was known to have a great affection for trees, hardly any for statues. (Remember Benjy's voice in *The Sound and the Fury:* "Caddy smelled like trees . . . Caddy smelled like trees in the rain.") His family responded with outrage.

"I'm horrified about the magnolia tree and the statue," Faulkner's daughter, Jill Summers, told the aldermen. "Please honor my father's often repeated wish for privacy. I do not want the statue of my father put on the square or anywhere else."

Misunderstanding, mortification, impasse. So it has always been and always will be, when politicians try to pay their respects to art. But the magnolia that knew William Faulkner lies dismembered in a landfill, and in our lifetime nothing—granite, bronze, or vegetable—will replace the shade or the dignity it supplied.

Trees have been much on my mind. The big machines have come to Hillsborough's old town cemetery, just beyond my garden fence, to clear the trees uprooted by a hurricane named Fran. The storm toppled nearly everything except a mammoth magnolia. A few months later the wretched village elders, citing their fear of another hurricane, sneaked into the cemetery at dawn and cut down that venerable magnolia, too.

For months two great trunks lay across a shattered stone wall, their roots gripping pieces of headstones and vaults, and dark fragments of wood that could have been ancient coffins. We looked away and looked back again, with morbid curiosity, anticipating something more alarming poking out of those red root-clots of clay.

A signer of the Declaration of Independence still rests just over the wall, along with an antebellum governor and a long roster of dignitaries buried here since the eighteenth century. But the cemetery isn't the place it was last summer, or for two hundred summers before that, when you could read the epitaphs or sit and read your book in the deepest, coolest, most poetic shade the township could provide. Direct sunlight looks rude and garish on mossy headstones that haven't felt the sun since Jeff Davis was president.

Maybe it's only our graves—after a century or two—that manage a dignity of their own. Stripped of trees, most of the real estate we trade and covet, most of the habitations of the human race look as dignified as Robert Dole in running shorts.

It was the most terrible year for the trees. A hurricane takes only an hour to accomplish a devastation that armies of savage developers couldn't manage in a decade. Raleigh, the City of Oaks, was altered forever by Fran, as Charleston was altered by Hugo. (Excuse Southern paranoia, but if it had been a northern state capital like Boston, or Harrisburg, Pennsylvania, the city's tragedy would have led every network newscast. To the New York media, hurricanes in the Carolinas are as remote and generic as typhoons in Bangladesh.)

I haven't dared to ask if the storm spared the Rose Garden, once my tree-rich sanctuary in the heart of Raleigh. But the hurricane's most catastrophic effects are out in the woods, far from the towns and traffic. The damage to my own property—two dozen trees destroyed or permanently disfigured—represented a small fraction of what this devil storm has cost me.

For years before I owned a house and trees, I rented them—in Wake, Durham, Orange, and Chatham counties. I rented some green and decent places, though my lot in North Raleigh was surrounded by bulldozers creating new subdivisions, and a pine grove in Durham where I read novels in perfect solitude is now the parking lot of the Sheraton. But mostly I appropriated places in parks and in the public forests, which usually belong to our universities. I always saw myself as a connoisseur of green places where a daydreamer could hide.

I can't explain why the loneliest places draw the wrath of the storm. Do buildings themselves act as windbreaks, is there a domino effect when the hurricane roars through a forest? But go see my favorite places for yourself. At UNC's Mason Farm in Chapel Hill, half of the old oak forest that inspired naturalist John K. Terres is lying in the swamp, or in chainsawed segments along the trail.

In the university's Botanical Gardens it was far worse. Hundreds of huge trees were stretched out in neat rows, like wheat straw behind a thresher. There's a place near the top of the hill, once forest, where no tree thicker than your wrist is still standing, for two hundred yards. In another place, a natural bowl, one of Fran's tornadoes uprooted every tree like a giant eggbeater.

The Duke Forest off Whitfield Road was a grim boneyard of fallen trees, and the scenic meanders of New Hope Creek are still choked with the storm's debris. In the elbow bend of the Eno River west of Hillsborough, my favorite grove of all, with twenty years of memories, was reduced to a natural clear-cut. The Eno, humiliated, flows sluggishly through a hopeless rubble of logs. When we walked the trail months later, even my dog seemed depressed.

They were my places. There are several I won't visit anymore. To me that feels very much like the death of a friend, or saying goodbye to one you don't expect to see again. Trees fall, cities spread. Rising generations, and future ones, will adjust to what they have, find shade where they can. Natural selection favors individuals who sleepwalk through whole seasons in city apartments, who would rather shop or Netsurf than walk three blocks to the park; who can live anywhere without really noticing, and never seek green sanctuary.

Spawned by nomadic company families, raised in subdivisions, they increasingly outnumber those of us from small towns, those of us from mountains who resonate to the prose of Edward Abbey (author, tree spiker, anarchist, onetime teacher at Western Carolina in Cullowhee) in *Appalachian Wilderness:* "The trees. Vegetation cradle of North America. All those trees transpiring patiently through the wet and exhilarating winds of spring, through the heavy, sultry, sullen summers into the smoky autumns. Through the seasons, years, millennia. . . . The hill country in North Carolina, eastern Kentucky and Tennessee seems today something like Punxsutawney, Pa., 50 years ago, or Home, Pa., where we grew up. All of it Appalachian, winter or summer, then or now. Land of the breathing trees, the big woods, the rainy forests." (True, Abbey migrated to the desert Southwest. But he earned his living as a fire lookout in the national forests.)

We'll soon be anachronisms, subjects like me who discover at a midway point in our lives that it was always trees, not houses, that constituted home. Anyone with enough money can have his house any way he chooses, even the way it looked in 1797. But trees are a legacy, subject to cancellation without notice, maintained with luck, love, faith, and vigilance. Some of the most fundamental grooves in our consciousness are formed by the way familiar trees divide, disperse, and define the daylight in which we live.

Think of coming home, after fifty years, to the place where you were raised. If all the trees are in place, you can imagine a vanished house more than adequately; if all the trees are gone, the house in its nakedness is just a pile of bricks and kindling. I'm unsentimental about the house where I grew up, because almost all my trees are gone—some condemned for such trivial sins as attracting squirrels. I recoil when I drive by my grandfather's house, sold out of the family forty years ago, where unspeakable barbarians cut down his whole orchard and his vineyards as well, replacing them with a single swing set on two acres now flat and featureless as a billiard table.

Call my condition arboreal dependency. In his brilliant book *Landscape and Memory,* Simon Schama argues that the psyches of great

nations—among them England, Germany, and the United States—
were formed in the forest primeval. England's morale has never fully
recovered, he suggests, from the great storm of 1703 that uprooted
seven thousand oaks in the New Forest and the Forest of Dean.

I believe it. In my front yard there's a seventy-foot hickory tree the
storm blew halfway over, before a maple broke its fall. It was the best
tree in my new yard. At irresponsible expense I hired some young
men with a towtruck to crank it nearly vertical, rebury its roots and
cable it in place.

The effect is not *Better Homes and Gardens*—five thick cables hold
it and the tree still leans at around eighty degrees. Some neighbors
called my disabled veteran "Crowther's Folly." Tourists pointed. But
one spring day there were new leaves on that hickory, and it was the
finest thing I had to celebrate all year.